PRAISE FOR AI LEADERS

"At no other time in this century has leadership been more critical to navigate, innovate, and implement AI tools with clarity and precision. Andreas demystifies complex concepts and equips leaders with the knowledge to harness AI's potential responsibly and innovatively. A must-read for those committed to leading at the forefront of AI integration and business transformation."

— ***Mary Purk,*** *Executive Director, AI at Wharton*

"Andreas Welsch has written a thoughtful guide to approaching AI. Essential reading for any organization and data & AI leaders who are trying to figure out how to navigate this rapidly evolving transformational technology to deliver meaningful business value to their company and their customers."

— ***Randy Bean,*** *Author of Fail Fast, Learn Faster: Lessons in Data Driven Leadership in an Age of Disruption, Big Data, and AI*

"Data and AI leaders need to be on eye-level with their C-Levels and advocate to challenge the hype. This book provides relevant insights that help data experts to grow into AI leaders."

— ***Dr. Michael Zimmer,*** *Chief Data & AI Officer, Insurance Industry*

"True AI leadership requires breaking down silos and fostering deep collaboration across the organization. Welsch's insights are invaluable."

— ***Bill Schmarzo,*** *Customer AI & Innovation Strategist, Dell Technologies*

"'Model' and 'Magic' are both 5-letter words beginning with 'M'. The secret to success is understanding the difference. Use this book to turn your models into action and avoid the traps of 'illusion'."

— ***T. Scott Clendaniel,*** *Director, Data & Analytics and AI, Gartner*

"Andreas' curiosity and eagerness to learn transformed our first interaction into a lasting friendship. Over the years, I've followed and actively engaged with his episodes on "What's the BUZZ?" The book delivers his insights to bridge the gap between technology and business as an essential guide to bring organizations along, identify the right opportunities, and set the proper guardrails."

— ***Harish Natarahjan,*** *Generative AI Industry Lead for High Tech, Accenture*

"An excellent resource for AI product managers and those looking to move into AI product roles to take a product-centric approach to AI."

— ***Supreet Kaur,*** *Data & AI Leader, Morgan Stanley*

"Andreas Welsch is a rare leader who combines a broad outlook with deep, tested insights. His expertise in AI is matched only by his brilliant, probing questions. Highly recommended."

— ***Lasse Rindom,*** *AI Lead, Basico P/S*

"Andreas captures the connection between technology and value in a book for business leaders written by a proven leader. His deep expertise in leadership took two directions: delivering technology and delivering solutions to customers. The combination allows Andreas to speak to all parts of the business."

— ***Vin Vashishta,*** *Founder & AI Strategy Advisor, V Squared*

"In a sea of AI hype, Welsch's relentless focus on the practical application of AI is refreshing."

— ***Brian Evergreen,*** *Author & Chief Executive Officer, The Future Solving Company*

"Don't let AI become just another shiny object. This book shows you how to make it work for you."

— ***Conor Grennan,*** *CEO, AI Mindset*

"Bringing AI to life in the enterprise is mostly about culture, people and processes and not about the technology. Welsch's book is a pragmatic AI blueprint any enterprise would be wise to follow."

— ***Mark Beccue,*** *Independent Market Analyst*

"For leaders weary of AI buzzwords, this book offers real substance with a proven framework to integrate AI capabilities throughout the enterprise. Struggling with AI terminology? This book clears the confusion and provides practical, actionable insights."

— ***Dalith Steiger-Gablinger,*** *Co-Founder, SwissCognitive AI Ventures, Advisory & Research*

AI LEADERSHIP HANDBOOK

AI LEADERSHIP HANDBOOK

A PRACTICAL GUIDE TO TURNING

TECHNOLOGY HYPE *INTO* **BUSINESS OUTCOMES**

ANDREAS WELSCH

AI LEADERSHIP HANDBOOK
A Practical Guide to Turning Technology Hype into Business Outcomes

Andreas Welsch

For more information: andreas@intelligence-briefing.com

ISBN (paperback): 978-1-962280-50-1
ISBN (ebook): 978-1-962280-51-8

Foreword

"If you wish to make an apple pie from scratch, you must first invent the universe."

—Carl Sagan

Professor Sagan's prescient quote aptly captures the challenges all of us, as humans, face when tasked with a practical problem. To create, to build, to bring anything novel into the world, requires first a deep contextual understanding of the landscape, the background, the environment into which our creation will reside. To put it more bluntly, we can't just wander into an enterprise, "sprinkle a little AI magic" on something, and hope for the best.

While the universe of Artificial Intelligence was conceived of generations ago, and doesn't necessarily need inventing, Andreas Welsch has provided readers of this handbook with the next best thing: a practical, approachable guide to the most pressing problems of the day, namely: how to recognize which problems should be solved by Artificial Intelligence (most of which is generative at this juncture), how to augment and upskill the people in your organizations so that their capabilities are amplified by this emergent technology, and how to leverage precious resources to positive effect in a responsible manner for those in and outside the organization.

Generative AI is one of the most exciting and promising fields of Artificial Intelligence, with applications ranging from art and music to medicine and engineering. But what does it mean for business strategists? How can they leverage Generative AI to create value, innovate, and compete in the rapidly changing world of the 21st century? And what are the challenges and opportunities that Generative AI poses for business leaders, organizations, and society at large?

This handbook aims to answer these questions and more, by providing a comprehensive and practical guide to AI for business strategists. It covers the basics of AI, its history, current state, and future trends. It showcases the best practices and examples of how leading companies and organizations are using AI to solve real-world problems, generating new insights, and enhancing customer experiences. And it offers a strategic framework and methods for business strategists to apply AI to their own domains and contexts, from ideation and experimentation to implementation and evaluation.

I have worked in, around and deeply through the Artificial Intelligence space for over a decade. Some of my education is formal, through coursework and development experiences, building software, models and productionizing platforms in and across life sciences and healthcare. Most of that experience, while of interest to me, and of value to the groups with whom we partnered and served, pales in comparison to the outsized expectations and interest received since November 2022 with the introduction of ChatGPT. Colleagues who once had asked: "Will your AI be robust enough to solve this problem for me?" were now asking "Will your AI take my job?" and everything else in between.

Sounding a clear call of reason and pragmatism and offering enthusiastic insights tempered with a healthy grounding in ethical, responsible practice was Andreas Welsch. I was fortunate enough to join Andreas as a guest on his podcast to introduce the role of the Chief AI Officer, a position I've now been in for over a year, and we've stayed close since.

You have in your hands, on your digital reader, on your device, wherever, a direct path to Artificial Intelligence success in the current climate. With comprehensive reviews of key thematic concerns to business leaders, strategists, data scientists, policy makers, funders and other important stakeholders, Andreas has crafted a tome that is easy to read, easy to apply, and easy to reference. I have a literal pile of AI books on my bookcase, but this is one that I can quickly recommend to colleagues looking to "level up" in the space; well done, my friend.

Like most things, in reading, I'd encourage you to begin with the end in mind; if you have a project in mind, but haven't identified the how or the guardrails, the sections on responsible use, ethics and other such considerations may be an appropriate place to start. If you've already stood up an AI council, and they are looking for a first assignment for their book club, this could be a very worthwhile consideration.

In the era of augmented intelligence which we've recently entered, the models, the software, the platforms (and accompanying hardware) are essential to success in the competitive environment in which we operate. But, synergy is not possible if we don't bring our human colleagues along for the ride; this handbook makes collaboration, cooperation and co-creation possible and practical, even as so much is changing in the environment.

Rishad Tobaccowala, a well regarded business strategist and international executive, has suggested that Generative AI is not overhyped, it is, in fact, underhyped. It is a reality and a force that is reshaping the world as we know it. It is also a source of hope and inspiration, a catalyst for innovation and transformation, and a tool for empowerment and collaboration. It is up to us, as business strategists, as leaders, and as citizens, to make the most of it, to harness its power for good, and to shape its future for the better. This handbook makes that possible in ways aligned to our enterprise expectations and responsibilities. I hope you enjoy reading it as much as I have.

— ***Matt Lewis,*** *Chief Artificial and Augmented Intelligence Officer, Inizio Medical*

About the Author

Andreas Welsch *is an internationally recognized AI leader, advisor, and speaker known for helping the world's leading enterprises turn technology hype into business outcomes.*

He is the Founder and Chief AI Strategist at Intelligence Briefing. Most recently, in global leadership roles at SAP, he has advised Fortune 500 leaders on realizing business value from AI, accelerated the integration of AI across enterprise applications, and positioned SAP as the leader for Business AI. Before that, Andreas led global IT process automation projects. Outside of work, he contributes to academia as an Adjunct Professor at West Chester University of Pennsylvania and serves on the Editorial Board of the Journal of AI, Robotics and Workplace Automation.

Andreas is a frequent keynote speaker and expert panelist and has been named a LinkedIn Top Voice, Thinkers360's Top 10 Thought Leader in Artificial Intelligence and Generative AI, SwissCognitive's Top 50 Global AI Ambassador, and engatica's Top 200 Worldwide Business & Technology Innovator. Follow his live stream & podcast, *What's the* BUZZ? and subscribe to his newsletter, *The AI MEMO*. If you want to work with Andreas to turn hype into outcome for your business, you can find him at www.intelligence-briefing.com.

Contents

Who Should Read This Book

If you are a current or aspiring technology leader, this book is for you. Especially if you lead a team or are part of one focusing on selecting, evaluating, implementing, or consulting on AI projects, you will find valuable learnings that you can apply in your organization. There is no single business function or team solely working on AI. If you work in a department such as data, data science and artificial intelligence, analytics, product development, or information technology, you will already have a foundation for running technology-focused projects and have likely come across some of the challenges addressed in this book.

Whether you are a manager, director, C-Level executive, or founder, the pressure to introduce more AI in your business applies across the board. Even if these aspects don't fit you, but you are interested in how leaders can successfully implement AI in their businesses, you will get a lot of value out of this book.

This book prepares you to lead AI programs in your business. It provides you with current approaches to AI leadership and an overview of relevant technology concepts. However, this book is not a guide to prompting large language models or a deep dive into individual technical topics, tools, or frameworks.

Introduction

AI has been a topic of fascination for decades. From Hollywood science-fiction stories to basic research, AI has undergone several hype cycles and so-called winters over the years and decades since the initial conference at Dartmouth in 1956[1]. The latest hype, fueled by Generative AI, is bringing the topic again onto the C-Suite agenda. That's great news for anyone working in the field. Because hype typically unlocks budget, funding, and resources. Executives rush to lead with AI projects, driven by their fear of missing out (FOMO), stories they see in the headlines and trade publications, and even what Hollywood portrays in their movies. Market research and economic impact studies aim to capture AI's potential on the global economy in astronomical heights—as much as entire economies. Although innovation management is well understood and taught, many companies still lack an innovation muscle, and this demand and pressure create a challenging situation.

1 McCarthy, John, Marvin L. Minsky, 1955, "A Proposal for the Dartmouth Summer Research Project on Artificial Intelligence."

In business, more often than not, AI is seen as a technology problem. But in fact, it is a people problem first. It touches on how people work and how they are used to working, which requires considerable change management. In addition to the focus on the microcosm of business, AI is even becoming a societal problem, given the pace of innovation and change. That again influences business and future jobs, from augmentation to automation and replacement. But despite the hype and excitement in the market and the need for increased digitalization, most AI projects in business fail. But why? After all, these businesses do have historical data—they most likely experimented with or rolled out Machine Learning, established IT departments, and already had innovation processes in place. The problem is multi-faceted. It is not just a matter of data alone or even of technology. Leaders need to get *every* dimension right. Just focusing on one or two, such as organizational culture and data privacy, means neglecting the others. That will lead to failure. However, most current and aspiring AI leaders are going through this monumental innovation for the first time in their career and are trying to "figure it out." What are the best approaches to determine and prioritize AI scenarios? How can we get support for building AI products across the business? How do we ensure the AI products we build are fair and free of bias? The uncertainty of this situation frequently leads to mistakes and missed opportunities they could avoid.

The recent hype around Generative AI is opening doors to boardrooms and C-Suites. Simultaneously, it pressures data and AI teams and their leaders to find the holy grail of revenue generation or process optimization. Yet, fundamental challenges, such as aligning AI with business strategy, focusing investments on products with demonstrable business value, and optimizing data and access to it, remain unresolved; hence, the chances are high that the latest wave of AI initiatives won't deliver the results that the AI hype promises. As of 2024, Generative AI is a promising technology still in its infancy and won't replace existing statistical methods anytime soon. Therefore, this book addresses both AI and Generative AI projects.

Where Should You Begin If You Want to Set Up AI in Your Business?

To understand better how leaders approach AI across different industries and company sizes, I started a live stream & podcast, *What's the* BUZZ?, in which my guests share their expertise and perspective on the episode's topic. Since the beginning of 2022, I have interviewed 62 leaders and hands-on practitioners on the show. *What's the* BUZZ? has a growing audience in 70 countries across the globe, with ever-increasing popularity and engagement, 50,000+ viewers and counting. My guests cover various viewpoints on leading AI programs in business: Chief AI Officer, Data Science Leader, Management Consultant, Academic, Ethicist, Founder, MLOps Engineer, Automation Expert, and more.

The thing that's become clear is this: successfully implementing AI in a business needs more than just good intentions. Business leaders will want to jump into starting AI projects. But without a clear goal and alignment with your business strategy, these AI projects will become money pits quickly without a return on investment in the future. However, if the AI strategy is aligned, the question of which AI features to prioritize remains. Without that definition, organizations chase projects opportunistically or based on quick wins that will likely not be as quick and successful as initially assumed.

However, the most well-aligned and prioritized use cases won't deliver the promised business value if technology and business teams don't communicate well. Implementing AI in isolation leads to inadequate use in production at best. Neglecting to include strong ethics practices in the decision and review process leads to biased results and amplifies imbalances at scale. Yet, even the best AI use cases won't find broader adoption if the teams who are supposed to use them live in a culture of skepticism and resistance.

Therefore, the leader's role is to shape an AI innovation culture and build up early adopters (*multipliers*) who act as liaisons in individual business functions. These multipliers can also act as a roll-in mechanism for pursuing new AI ideas. However, AI initiatives in a business will have an impact only through the combination of these elements. Three fundamental aspects stand out: leadership, organization, and responsibility. This book covers nine themes discussed in the *What's the* BUZZ*?* live stream & podcast as well as the newsletter *The AI MEMO*:

hype & expectations, strategy, leadership, product mindset, culture, collaboration, ethics & sustainability, technology, and data privacy & security.

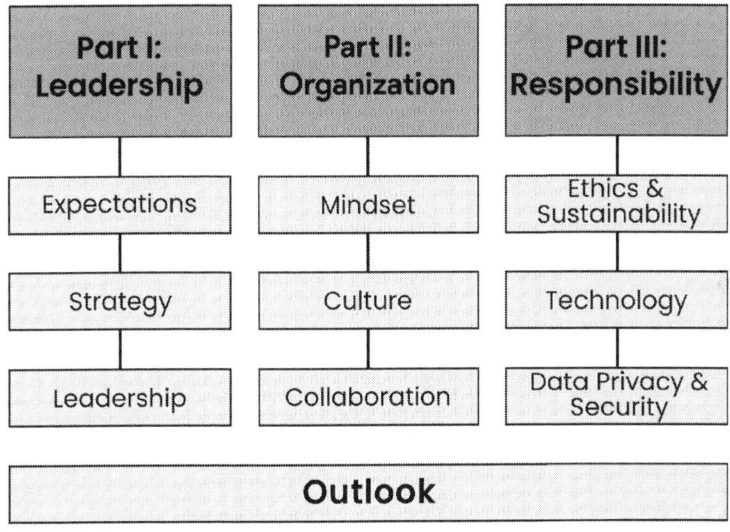

Dimensions of Successful AI Initiatives

The pressure on leaders to incorporate AI into their business has never been higher. Between unrealistic expectations of what AI can do, isolated science projects turned into money pits, and employees looking for clarity on how AI influences their jobs, learning how to successfully introduce AI into your organization can be difficult. Getting it right on the second or third attempt is not an option. In order for your AI initiative to be successful, you need to be aware of all the facets involved, not just the technology—a daunting task. This book prepares you to master the nine most important facets with ease. In these chapters, you will learn how to:

- Leverage the full scope of an AI leadership role
- Win (enthusiastic) buy-in from employees
- Take a product-centric approach to building AI applications
- Build a pipeline of high-value AI capabilities
- Utilize AI ethically, safely, and sustainably

Spanning strategy, stakeholder management, collaboration, culture, ethics, data privacy, risk management, and technology, you will learn everything you need to know to become a confident and successful AI leader—and get your AI initiative right on the first try. In Part I, we'll delve into the foundation of AI leadership. From exploring the forces that drive the AI hype to aligning business and AI strategy, and guiding the business transformation, you will get insights that prepare you to lead AI initiatives in your business.

In Part II, we explore how, in your AI leadership role, you can enable your organization for successful AI adoption—and that depends on people. It all begins with taking a product-centric mindset that puts users first, fostering a culture of innovation within your organization, and supporting collaboration between your technical and business teams.

In Part III, we discuss core aspects of building AI products responsibly. This includes defining and operationalizing your organization's AI ethics policy, evaluating current data and technology practices, and evolving your data privacy and risk management.

Lastly, the book closes with an outlook of emerging capabilities and concepts in the rapidly evolving field of AI such as agents and multi-modal models. The further reading section at the end of each chapter includes references to books that live stream guests have published so you can further deepen your understanding of individual topics. The Appendix lists details about the 62 guests, including links to the live stream and podcast episodes that are the basis for this book. Watch or listen at your own pace at www.intelligence-briefing.com.

Whether you are currently in an AI leadership role or are aspiring to move into one, this book will prepare you to turn technology hype into business outcomes. But before you can understand where AI is now and where it's going, you need to know where it started.

Part I

BUILDING LEADERSHIP FOUNDATIONS

AI is in the middle of a hype[1]. Vendors herald it as the next innovation comparable to humankind's discovery of fire. Investors are pouring money into startups that promise to drive this revolution. Leaders across all business functions are seeing its effects: customers, partners, and boards are pushing senior leaders to identify ways to incorporate AI into their business operations to increase efficiencies, capture new markets, and raise shareholder value. While Generative AI is novel as a technology, exploring its best use in a business and prioritizing investments still needs to follow tried approaches and processes. AI leaders are critical in this process and must align their AI efforts with

---

1 Gartner, 2024, "Hype Cycle for Artificial Intelligence," June 17, 2024, https://www.gartner.com/en/documents/5505695.

the business strategy. Pursuing AI for the sake of AI is a sure way to money pits, sunk costs, and missed opportunities. To avoid these issues, a new role has emerged to align all AI-related efforts across the company. This role is the Chief AI Officer. The scope of this role extends beyond technology and establishing AI as an essential capability of the company and spans creating first pilot projects to upskilling the workforce on AI. This section of the book demonstrates the foundations of AI leadership for successfully implementing AI in business.

Chapter One

THE FORCES THAT DRIVE AI

To understand the hype around AI, one needs to know how innovations permeate industries and businesses. Innovation management theory describes innovation in 45-60-year-long waves called Kondratiev Waves. Named after their Soviet economist creator, Kondratiev Waves are long transformational developments that have enabled industrialization, mobility, and connectivity. The first half of the 19th century brought coal and steam engines, which helped societies to produce goods and move upward. The second half of the century saw the emergence of steel as a building material instead of iron and the first long-distance mobility and transportation via railways. In the first half of the 20th century, the advent of electricity allowed businesses and households to keep the lights on, and discoveries in chemistry created the foundation of quantum mechanics and synthetic polymers such as nylon. And the second half of the 20th century saw personal mobility via automobiles skyrocket. In the last decade of the century and the beginning of the 21st century, transformative innovations such as computers, the internet, and smartphones became household goods. Experts agree that AI is the next wave in this line. Its impact will be magnitudes more significant than previous ones and overlap with the IT cycle. Given innovation's pace and impact, the latest innovation cycles, such as AI, are becoming much shorter.

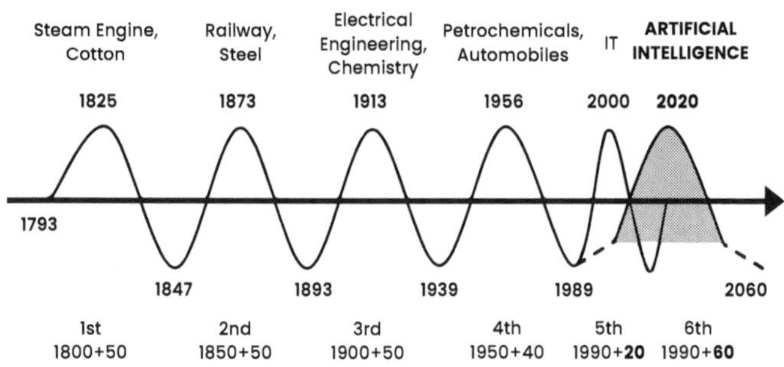

Kondratiev Waves of Innovation[2]

Consequently, AI will be more readily available, quickly adopted, and widely used. But AI is just a technology. It's just a tool of little value by itself. AI is only impactful when

2 Adapted from Andreas J. W. Goldschmidt, 2004, "Research | International Healthcare Management Institute," 2004, https://www.uni-trier.de/index.php?id=28954.

applied in a context—such as business. Although the current wave of Generative AI is bringing AI to the forefront of business decisions, the hype around AI did not start in 2022—in truth, it began decades before.

Understanding the History of AI Hype

We are witnessing the latest AI hype. AI promises to do things that humans can do, but do them better, faster, and cheaper, for example: processing information. Additionally, it can even do things we are not good at or simply can not do. Naturally, leaders across industries and geographies seek ways to harness it in their business. But the AI hype did not just start in the winter of 2022 or even the mid-2010s. It dates back to the 1956 *Dartmouth Summer Research Project on Artificial Intelligence*, organized by researcher Marvin Minsky at Dartmouth College. This event was the birth moment of AI.

The project sought to explore how machines could act on human instructions. Many of the tenets of AI that the researchers defined back then remain relevant to this day. The most notable principles are natural language processing (NLP), neural networks, and the theory of computation, abstraction, and creativity. In the mid-1950s, several names existed for the concept of AI, such as *thinking machines*. Due to its neutrality, Minsky's peer, John McCarthy, proposed the term *Artificial Intelligence (AI)*. The researchers who contributed to the project believed machines would be as intelligent as humans within a decade. That didn't quite happen. Technology and data hit several roadblocks. As a result, governments in the United States and the United Kingdom cut back their funding, redirecting it to projects that yielded faster outcomes from about 1974-1980.

The 1980s saw the creation of so-called *expert systems*. These systems have encoded and encapsulated the knowledge of human experts. However, like several times before, the expectations surpassed reality by orders of magnitude. As a result, funding dried up, and people moved on to different topics again from approximately 1987 until 2000. These periods of reduced funding and focus are also known as *AI winters*.

The 2010s brought renewed interest in AI. The industry focused on a sub-discipline called *Machine Learning (ML)*, a capability by which software analyzes and detects patterns in vast amounts of data and creates a representation of these patterns, aka a *model*. These models mimic aspects of the human brain, so-called *neural networks* that process information and make predictions. In business, this could be classifying incoming emails into *spam* or *no spam* in IT, product recommendations in e-commerce, or fraud detection in finance.

By the mid-2010s, three critical factors were now finally present that enabled the rise of ML: vast amounts of data required to build models (big data), the ability to process this data using massively parallel processing (GPUs), and the ability to do both with scale and elasticity (cloud computing). But another ingredient still needed to be included. ML promised to revolutionize the business world. It was a hype. Business leaders poured money into proofs-of-concept and custom models. These models were supposed to deliver an edge over their business's competition. However, to build an ML model, companies needed highly skilled and highly paid experts (data scientists) in addition to usable data and clearly defined objectives. These prerequisites raised the entry barrier to ML for small- and medium-sized businesses. And just because the talent was available in-house didn't automatically mean every project would succeed. ML was simply *unavailable to the masses*—companies and consumers alike. In 2018, market analyst firms like Gartner[3] estimated that about 85% of ML projects fail to deliver the expected outcome. Management consulting powerhouse McKinsey & Company[4] found in 2022 that only 50% of businesses use AI in at least one of their business functions. The hype was waning despite the technology's potential, the pressure to innovate, and the leaders' promptness to invest. By the end of 2022, it was turning into disillusionment and, for some, even despair. The first tech observers discussed whether the next *AI winter* was near. But one aspect had gone unnoticed.

---

3 Gartner, 2018, "Gartner Says Nearly Half of CIOs Are Planning to Deploy Artificial Intelligence," February 13, 2018, https://www.gartner.com/en/newsroom/press-releases/2018-02-13-gartner-says-nearly-half-of-cios-are-planning-to-deploy-artificial-intelligence.

4 McKinsey & Company, 2022, "The state of AI 2022 — and half a decade in review." December 6, 2022, https://www.mckinsey.com/capabilities/quantumblack/our-insights/the-state-of-ai-in-2022-and-a-half-decade-in-review.

Around the summer of 2020, OpenAI, a startup out of the US Pacific Northwest, had already released its latest model, GPT-3. This model was different from traditional ML and Deep Learning algorithms. It was based on a new architecture of neural networks, so-called *transformers*, introduced by researchers at Google[5]. For example, unlike previous approaches, transformers take text input and put words into context with each other rather than just making predictions about the next word. The type of AI model often using transformers is the so-called *foundation model* (for its foundational capabilities for software development), introduced by researchers at Stanford University[6]. Foundation models such as GPT-3 could process instructions such as *"Explain what an NDA is in the language of a 5-year-old."* It's an example of Generative AI, a new kind of AI. For the first time in the history of computing, an application could generate information, not just predict values. This technology is a significant reason for the decreasing cost of information generation and summarization. The effects of the cost of information converging toward zero can be good and bad depending upon the affected subpopulations. One thing is certain, though: It will affect knowledge economies today and in the years to come.

---

5 Vaswani, Ashish, et al., 2017, "Attention is all you need," June 12, 2017, https://arxiv.org/abs/1706.03762.

6 Bommasami, Rishi, et al., 2021, "On The Opportunities And Risks Of Foundation Models," August 16, 2021, https://arxiv.org/abs/2108.07258.

Oftentimes, people overestimate the short-term impact and underestimate the long-term impact—at least until a hype and an adopting majority are forming. Early examples of Generative AI before the hype has taken off include generating images (OpenAI DALL-E and Midjourney) and text (OpenAI GPT-3). Most people viewed these models as a novelty until OpenAI released ChatGPT on November 30, 2022. The reception had been similar during the first weeks since its initial release to the public ("novelty"). However, along with a growing number of users came the increasing realization that this technology could be a significant leap forward in AI. Within two months of its release, ChatGPT had become the fastest-growing software application, with more than 200 million monthly active users. Business leaders realized quickly that the underlying technology promised significant productivity gains and revenue opportunities. In 2023, additional Generative AI models, such as audio and video, have gained popularity. The latest advancement is multi-modality, a model's ability to generate different media types and take one kind of media to generate another.

Along with all of these advances, the term Artificial Intelligence has become inflationary. Whether to meet market, investor, or customer expectations, it risks diluting its actual meaning. AI refers to sophisticated systems and probabilistic models that recognize patterns in data, categorize information, or identify outliers. These methods were previously also known as Machine Learning.

This book adopts the following distinction between Artificial Intelligence, Machine Learning, Deep Learning, and Generative AI:

- Artificial Intelligence is the broader domain and software capability.
- Machine Learning is a sub-discipline of AI focused on recognizing patterns in data.
- Deep Learning is a sub-discipline of ML, concerned with the learning aspect of ML by methods such as neural networks.
- Generative AI is based on Deep Learning and is focused on generating information.

Whenever you see the respective terms Machine Learning, Deep Learning, and Generative AI, they will refer to the specifics of their technology. Whenever you see the term AI, it is a reference to the broader field, encompassing all of the different technologies underneath, including Generative AI.

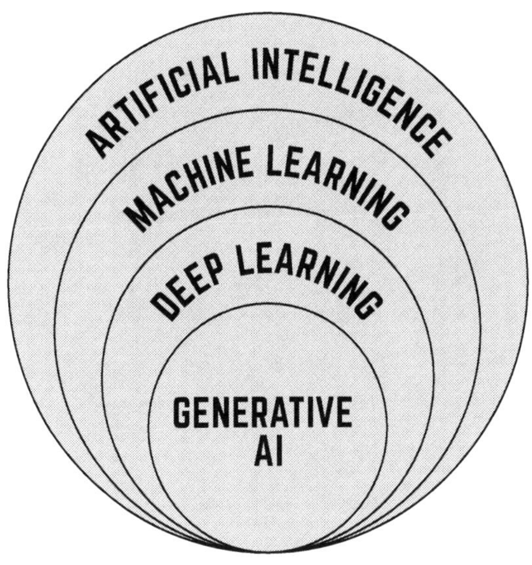

Artificial Intelligence and Related Terminology

Describing What's Special About Generative AI

When discussing Generative AI, the most common question is, *"What makes Generative AI so different from previous AI generations?"* To build a model, one has always needed to have data. One has always had to identify and reduce bias to ensure the fairness of its predictions. One has always had to put it into a business context. So what's new? Observing the adoption of Generative AI, four dimensions make Generative AI different:

1. **Access:** Generative AI is available to anyone with an internet connection. To be a user, you no longer need a supercomputer, a powerful server, or a computer. You can use Generative AI applications at home or

on the go, for example, from your smartphone. On top of that, most software providers offer a free trial version of their product or charge a low monthly fee. This combination makes Generative AI much more accessible than previous generations of AI.

2. **Quality:** Generative AI models' output is often tough to distinguish from a human-created equivalent. The generated text sounds as if a human had written it. Generated images of people and places depict reality, although the person or place does not exist. Generated, "synthetic" voices sound like a voice actor has recorded them, although they have not. Generated videos may give the impression of reality, but they are created using Generative AI. Therefore, it is becoming significantly harder for humans to tell truth from tale.
3. **Scale:** Previous innovation waves have brought global internet and social media connectivity. Due to that worldwide connectivity, anyone can instantly share any AI-generated output globally and reach billions of people within seconds.
4. **Impact:** Because of the above three points, the effect of Generative AI can have unforeseen consequences (good and bad). Vulnerable parts of the population are especially at risk of taking AI-generated content at face value and might act upon it. These circumstances pose societal, political, and security threats.

Let's look at three examples to address any reservations and illustrate the observation.

> **Example 1:** "People have always photoshopped."
> That might be true. But previously, humans needed access to the software (which was costly or resource-intensive) and the skills to create high-quality results.
> **Example 2:** "People have always created and shared lies."
> That might be true. However, fabricating high-quality evidence, *scaling* it, and sharing it with a broad range of people previously required much work.
> **Example 3:** "Software has always automated decision-making."
> That might be true. But previously, it has required humans to *explicitly define* every operation they wanted the software to take over.

As you set up your AI program, establish guidelines for using Generative AI in your business and evaluate Generative AI use cases, you will encounter at least one of these four dimensions in any situation. For example:

- What are the risks to information security if anyone in your business can use Generative AI? This involves updating information security policies, tools, and training to prevent data leakage.

- How important are authenticity and traceability in content creation for your business? The answer will vary depending on what your teams use Generative AI for. Copy for your website is most likely less critical than generating images with consumer-grade tools and using the output for ad campaigns.
- What are the consequences if this AI feature goes sideways? Due to its global scale, the risks can be significant, whether it is reputational damage through viral social media threads or impacting your users through incorrect or false information.
- What is the impact of AI-generated information for your customers? The answer will vary whether it is an internal IT chatbot or a customer-facing mental health assistant.

In addition, you should also evaluate existing guidelines and processes against these four dimensions to see if any adjustments are needed to cover Generative AI. Your Generative AI policy should include:

- Tools permitted for use
- Information classification
- Recommendations for output use
- Education about limitations

Generative AI introduces several new aspects. However, most of those you needed to get right before the emergence of Generative AI remain relevant, whether you pursue ML, AI, Generative AI, or even other types of process automation. Generative AI does not negate or make the learnings of the previous AI hype obsolete—quite the opposite. For example, companies still need to identify and prioritize the most promising AI scenarios to pursue. The need to determine a scenario's business value and return on investment remains. Similarly, businesses still need data to enrich Large Language Models (LLM) and their output. That data needs to be available, accessible, clean, and complete to be useful for AI. Stakeholder and change management are also among your capabilities as an AI leader which are critical to ensure buy-in by senior leaders and employees who will work with the AI products your AI team develops. In fact, these learnings are the foundation upon which organizations can build. We will cover them in the subsequent chapters.

Realizing AI's Potential Impact on Labor and Economies

The promise is simple. It's as old as the idea of progress: a new technology helps us reduce or eliminate a mundane task. We've seen it repeatedly and benefit from large and small innovations in all aspects of our lives—as consumers and professionals. What's interesting, though, is that what is mundane changes as the level of automation increases and technology evolves. Most recently, we have seen the promise of reducing mundane tasks with the help of AI and automation. But does it mean we are eliminating all mundane tasks in a business?

Transformational technologies have historically led to shifts in labor and roles. In the 1400s, scribes would write books. The capacity to publish and share knowledge was constrained. With the invention of the printing press by Johannes von Gutenberg in 1439, the publishing of ideas and information now happened at a much faster pace and scale, enabling movements such as Reformation and Protestantism in Europe. Ultimately, the typesetting and printing process transformed with the availability of computers. Typesetting, a manual process until then, was being replaced by increased automation. Print media, such as actual newspapers, has been transforming into entirely digital publishing, leading to the consolidation and demise of several formerly well-known publishing houses. But it's not all about just print and media:

- **Communication:** Switchboard operators have been replaced with hardware, enabled by the transistor and integrated circuits.
- **Banking:** Bank tellers have been replaced with Automated Teller Machines (ATMs).
- **Travel:** Travel agents have been replaced with self-service portals online and airline websites.
- **Retail:** Cashiers have partially been replaced with connected Point of Sale (POS) systems and self-checkout lines.

When tasks like these no longer need to be executed by a person, it leads to increased levels of automation and the next set of tasks being viewed as mundane:

Take the accounts payable process within finance, from identifying which invoice to pay, to whom, and how much to authorizing the payment. Without any automation, finance team members manually log into the vendor's invoice portal to download the latest invoices, open the invoice on their computer, copy & paste the invoice number, date, amount, and other fields into their finance application, send a note to the vendor that they will make the payment for the following invoices and amount, and authorize the payment.

In recent years, finance teams have increased the level of automation, leading to increased efficiency:

- **Phase 1:** Using a Robotic Process Automation (RPA) bot, the finance team automates logging in to the vendor invoice portal and downloading the invoice. A finance team member then opens the invoice document and transfers the information into the finance application.
- **Phase 2:** In addition to the scope of Phase 1, the team now increases the level of automation to process the invoice and extract relevant information by using a combination of Optical Character Recognition and ML. The technology identifies the characters on a page and puts them into a business context (e.g. vendor name, invoice date, invoice number, amount). Next, the RPA bot enters that information into the finance application. The finance team member writes an email to the vendor that they will shortly make the payment

and copies & pastes information about the invoices and total amount into the email.

- **Phase 3:** Building on Phase 2, the finance team can now also generate the email body to send to the vendor with the help of Generative AI, automatically filling in the previously extracted information about the invoices to be paid. The finance team reviews the email draft, presses "Send," and authorizes the payment.

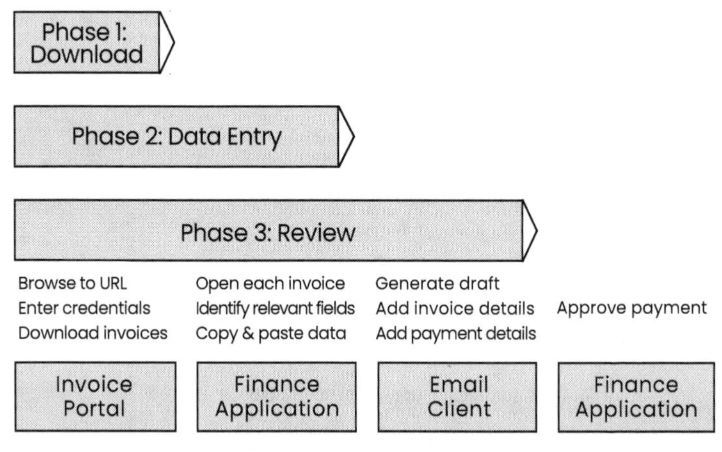

Evolution of Mundane Tasks

In this illustrative example, the finance team member moves from data entry to reviewing information while mundane tasks in this process, such as obtaining documents, identifying and extracting relevant information, entering the information, and sending an email, are progressively automated. After automating the mundane task of logging in and downloading an invoice, manually identifying and extracting information becomes the new mundane task, until that is automated.

For business functions such as IT, introducing automation creates a new set of tasks that are mundane again, for example monitoring and maintaining the tools and technologies that perform this automation in a shift of labor from the business towards IT and Centers of Excellence (CoE) who have created and have had to maintain the software that now automates that task.

Traditionally, this has led to reskilling and upskilling of people in these roles that have become redundant because of more advanced technology and automation. One of the most significant and hotly debated aspects of Generative AI is its impact on the workforce. Any kind of automation has always sought to automate mundane, repetitive tasks. IT-supported finance processes have replaced paper-based methods of accounting. Software robots have replaced copy-and-paste tasks of downloading, processing, and uploading invoices. But, this time, it is also about automating white-collar jobs. In 2023, Goldman Sachs[7] published a study about the economic impact of Generative AI. Their predictions reference an effect on 300 million jobs worldwide.

---

7 Goldman Sachs, 2023, "Generative AI Could Raise Global GDP by 7%," April 5, 2023, https://www.goldmansachs.com/intelligence/pages/generative-ai-could-raise-global-gdp-by-7-percent.html.

Similarly, McKinsey & Company[8] have estimated that Generative AI will contribute to a $2.6-4.4 trillion increase in the global GDP. That is the equivalent of the economy of France ($3 trillion) or even Germany ($4.3 trillion). While these numbers sound impressive, they also lead to humans' fear of mass unemployment if AI takes over more tasks than before. Unlike previous generations of AI, Generative AI has the potential to impact white-collar roles more disproportionately—for example, creatives, marketing, clerks, and lawyers.

Another study by Boston Consulting Group and Wharton School of Business[9] has found that Generative AI tools support employees with lower levels of proficiency in a domain more strongly than those already more proficient. Businesses must incorporate AI into their operations and continuous innovation to benefit from this productivity boost and democratization of skills. For most companies, this is much more challenging than it sounds. Established processes and practices are complex to change for three reasons: the cost of doing so, the risk and impact of failure, and people's preference for stability.

---

8 McKinsey & Company, 2023, "The economic potential of Generative AI: The next productivity frontier," June 14, 2023, https://www.mckinsey.com/capabilities/mckinsey-digital/our-insights/the-economic-potential-of-generative-ai-the-next-productivity-frontier.

9 Boston Consulting Group, 2023, "How People Can Create—and Destroy—Value with Generative AI," September 21, 2023, https://www.bcg.com/publications/2023/how-people-create-and-destroy-value-with-gen-ai.

Senior business leaders often view AI as a one-time project and communicate that expectation to you if you are on point for delivering these projects. Unfortunately, this expectation couldn't be further from reality. A one-and-done approach to AI leads to missed opportunities when the underlying model's performance degrades due to a shift in new data and behavior or to higher ramp-up cost if a new team needs to be assembled and enabled for a follow-on project. AI is a constant effort that needs sustained focus, investment, and improvement. It is a journey rather than a destination. Therefore, you must set up and help guide businesses on that journey. To do this successfully, you need more than just technical skills or domain expertise in a business area. You must be able to navigate both technical and business conversations if you want to succeed. As an AI leader, you must be a trusted partner to the technology teams and the business. Your first task in the new role is to define the company's AI strategy. But where should you start?

In the next chapter, we will review how an effective AI strategy comes about and the dependencies on other organizational dynamics and objectives.

Key Takeaways

In this chapter, we've set the scene for the current AI hype and its origins:

- AI is a crucial basic technology of our time. Its beginnings trace back to the 1950s.

- Scientists and business leaders have repeatedly promised they are about to reach an inflection point soon—only to correct themselves.
- Generative AI is a new kind of AI technology that can create information such as text, image, audio, and video. There is renewed hype surrounding Generative AI.
- Transformative technologies have historically led to changes in the labor market. However, as existing jobs were no longer needed, new ones emerged, providing opportunities to those who have adapted.
- Business leaders should treat AI as a continuous effort rather than a discrete project.

Further Reading

- Gilmurray, Kieran and Olivier Gomez. 2024. *The A-Z Of Generative AI: A Guide To Leveraging AI For Business.* 979-8884838604.
- Bean, Randy. 2021. *Fail Fast, Learn Faster: Lessons in Data-Driven Leadership in an Age of Disruption, Big Data, and AI.* Wiley. 978-1119806226.
- Bornet, Pascal, Ian Barkin, and Jochen Wirtz. 2020. *Intelligent Automation: Learn how to harness Artificial Intelligence to boost business & make our world more human.* 979-8691819230.

Chapter Two

ALIGNING AI WITH BUSINESS GOALS

To successfully deploy AI technologies, it is essential for business leaders to adapt classic management principles for the age of AI. ChatGPT, Midjourney, and the like have made AI more accessible to a broader audience. Most of the current Generative AI models use text-based input such as chats or written instructions (aka *prompts*). This input type is a significant leap forward compared to previous AI and ML generations, which leverage statistics. Tools such as ChatGPT and Midjourney simplify interacting with the technology and let anyone achieve outcomes quickly without any underlying data science, statistics, or math knowledge. Hence, leaders outside core technology domains can also experience it for themselves. They can see it, try it out, and share it.

Therefore, a company's investors, analysts, and customers are asking the senior leadership team how they will leverage this technology—to increase efficiency, provide better customer service, create entirely new products and business models, and increase revenue. These demands create additional pressure at a time when most businesses are already behind on AI adoption or just starting on their journey. The pressure will trickle down to you as the AI leader. However, the leap from simply using ChatGPT to identifying and implementing business use cases that deliver measurable value can be significant.

Business leaders new to AI often view it as a technology play, considering it a part of the technology team's responsibility—*a solution looking for a problem*. However, the technology itself is just a secondary aspect. It is a means to an end. Before starting an AI journey, leaders must know what business objectives they want to achieve—and only then start looking at AI to identify potential solutions. That is why the classic management principles still apply to AI as well:

- "A company's vision and mission should be revisited and refreshed periodically to ensure they remain relevant and aligned with the company's evolving goals." (Clayton Christensen, 1997)
- "Culture eats strategy for breakfast." (Attributed to Peter Drucker)
- "Structure follows strategy." (Alfred Chandler, 1962)

AI must align with the mission and vision of any business to be an effective technology. You already have a business strategy (unless you're starting a new business). Your C-Suite has defined it in the past. Your company is diligently following it and measuring success. Then, along comes an exogenous event, such as a new technology. This technology has the potential to turn your industry upside down. It's revolutionary, transformative, and disruptive. Incumbents are incorporating it into their products, and your competitors are jumping at the opportunity to evaluate and implement it. This event triggers your C-Suite to revisit your business strategy, to adjust to what the market is doing, what your competitors are up to, and what the new technology can do for your business.

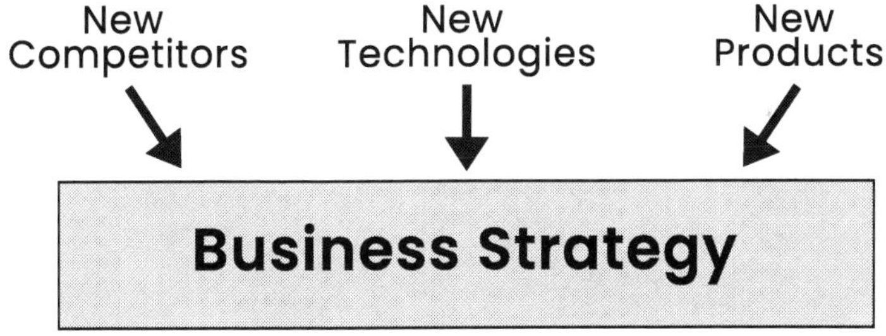

External Events Influencing Business Strategy

Most recently, the emergence of Generative AI has created such an event, initiating a wave of change. This change will impact every business and every industry—including the one you are in. But this was anything but certain, because AI was actually on a downward trend at the end of 2022. According to

McKinsey & Company's report, *The State of AI 2022*[10], adoption was flattening at 50-60% across the companies surveyed. But Generative AI has propelled AI back onto the C-Suite's agenda. It has become easier for anyone to experiment with tools such as OpenAI ChatGPT, Microsoft Bing, or Google Gemini. Therefore, C-Level leaders are also asked by their boards and peers what their AI strategy is.

Vision & Mission

Business Strategy

AI Strategy

Technology Strategy | Data Strategy

Grounding AI Strategy in the Business Strategy

10 McKinsey & Company, 2022, "The state of AI 2022 — and half a decade in review," December 6, 2022, https://www.mckinsey.com/capabilities/quantumblack/our-insights/the-state-of-ai-in-2022-and-a-half-decade-in-review.

For any AI initiative to be successful, it needs to fit into the larger context of strategies. Its main goal is to support the business strategy. Therefore, you must develop the AI strategy in collaboration with other business leaders and break it down from the business strategy to the technology and data strategy. If one aspect of the business strategy seeks to improve customer loyalty by five percentage points, the AI strategy must support reaching it. It's that simple. An AI strategy alone won't do.

Leaders should develop a North Star for their business of where they want it to be 3-5 years from now and determine how AI will help them achieve that vision. This plan needs to encompass all business functions—from finance and HR to supply chain, warehousing, and customer service.

The flip side of AI's potential for your business is your leadership's expectations. Expectations are about as high as they can get, and you must manage them to deliver realistic results in a realistic time frame. A consistent and connected strategic approach will help give you the confidence to prioritize and pursue AI scenarios that align with your vision and help you get closer to achieving it. It will also assist you in declining to pursue use case ideas that do not fit into your strategy and provide you with the backup context for your decision.

Where leaders place their bets is as critical for pursuing AI as any other strategic business decision. That means understanding the competitive landscape of the business and who could disrupt it. Due to the rapid growth and adoption of Generative AI tools, vendors such as OpenAI now own a new entry point or user experience (UX) layer on top of applications. End-users use applications such as OpenAI ChatGPT, Anthropic Claude, and Perplexity to research, summarize, and create information. Previously, searching for information has been a dominant feature of search engines such as Google Search or Microsoft Bing. Whoever controls the application through which end-users access information also controls the gateway to the services end-users can access. OpenAI is challenging the traditional online search paradigm and launched a prototype called SearchGPT in July 2024.[11] Offering additional capabilities like connections to partner services (e.g., via plug-ins) is likely the first step. Other capabilities, such as e-commerce or entertainment, could be future opportunities that leaders in these industries should have on their radar.

Therefore, they should ask themselves: *How will AI affect our industry? Can we create a competitive advantage? Is AI posing an existential threat to our business? How does this technology change the way we deliver value to our customers?* You can use this momentum to discuss how AI can contribute to your business's success. This circumstance presents a unique opportunity as business leaders typically want to learn about business outcomes rather than the underlying technology. But Generative AI is different. Many business leaders are using it themselves this time around. Their familiarity with AI as a topic will make it easier to

---

11 Reuters, 2024, "OpenAI enters Google-dominated search market with SearchGPT," July 26, 2024, https://www.reuters.com/technology/artificial-intelligence/openai-announces-ai-powered-search-tool-searchgpt-2024-07-25.

mobilize resources and budget across the business, and to create a convicted point of view on using AI.

Creating a Convicted Point of View

A common reaction by business leaders to the opportunity and threat of AI is to spin up pilot projects. Their goal is to assess the potential of AI for the business quickly. However, this approach frequently leads to sunk costs as these pilot projects prove an idea in a limited environment rather than being built to be transferred to production. These so-called *throw-away projects* often lack a clear strategy and executive sponsorship. Gartner[12] estimates that about 30% of Generative AI projects do not pass the proof-of-concept phase.

Instead of rushing toward AI and spinning up isolated pilot projects, leaders should develop a roadmap for how AI will support their business strategy.

Ideally, leaders go "all-in" on AI and create new business models with data and AI at their core. Historically, though, this has been significantly harder to achieve for established businesses running heterogeneous, legacy IT infrastructures, decade-old processes and workflows where change can disrupt the flow of business before it delivers outcomes. For these businesses, it is

---

12 Gartner, 2024, "Gartner Predicts 30% of Generative AI Projects Will Be Abandoned After Proof of Concept By End of 2025," July 29, 2024, https://www.gartner.com/en/newsroom/press-releases/2024-07-29-gartner-predicts-30-percent-of-generative-ai-projects-will-be-abandoned-after-proof-of-concept-by-end-of-2025.

a matter of identifying opportunities for introducing AI into existing processes and workflows while minimizing disruption. As AI continues to proliferate software, there will hardly be a product without it that your business teams use. Examples of introducing AI into existing operations are using marketing tools for generating content or stock images with AI, adding product recommendations to your e-commerce store, or offering an AI-enabled chatbot for HR questions to your end-users. These improvements are rather minor in scope and can still yield measurable benefits. While AI provides short-term benefits in these situations, you need to address the underlying, foundational data issues in order to achieve the full business benefits from AI.

On the other hand, those companies who can fully embrace AI beyond point solutions can capture significant value for themselves and their customers. They often change their existing business model around AI or create entirely new business models with AI being the central technology. These businesses have a C-Suite that goes beyond lip service and proclaiming to "do AI." The top-level leaders understand that AI needs to focus on more than just "quick wins," experimentations, or expanding existing solutions (aka *bolt-ons*). Instead, AI needs to permeate the entire organization. It affects every business function, domain, and position. It includes those teams that build AI products, those that use them, and those that sell them. Aside from organizational aspects, being an AI-centric business involves a strong focus on data—from capturing it to using it to drive decisions. Going "all-in" means creating value when processes are rethought from the ground up with data at their core, rather than sprinkling AI over a broken, decade-old business process.

When it comes to ideating the use of AI for their organization, many leaders use a bottom-up approach to gather ideas from subject-matter experts. They engage in innovation programs for innovation's sake and cannot transfer these innovations into their core products and services. The problem is that only a few of these ideas are measurable regarding business impact, value, and return on investment. Effective use of AI impacts a measurable business metric.

For example, pursuing a chat-based IT support use case might lead to "happier employees;" it's an admirable aspiration. However, it will be hard to quantify and measure in financial terms unless increasing employee satisfaction is one of your business goals and you can directly attribute introducing your AI feature to increasing employee satisfaction. Hence, it will be hard to justify the investment and its return to your senior leadership.

Selecting the Optimal Technology for the Business Problem

Despite all the hype around AI and the pressure on senior leadership to react, AI teams need to assess each AI use case idea carefully: *Should we solve this business problem with AI? Are there less complex and less expensive technologies or approaches we should be pursuing instead?* That first question is critical for setting the AI team up for success. Leaders often fall into the trap of looking for an AI approach to solving a problem rather than understanding the underlying business problem first. This intent frequently means that the AI team will spend time and resources on a problem they could solve more efficiently from a business perspective—for example, with process automation or rules that are explicitly defined. They typically do not require as much data or infrastructure, and thereby, are cheaper to build and operate. Keep in mind that not every business problem is an AI problem.

Humans have historically performed operational tasks themselves, such as forecasting demand, submitting orders, or closing the books. However, since the 1960s, business software has become available, increasing the level of automation and autonomy in performing these tasks. Understanding which technology to use and when to use it enables you to adequately select the one that most efficiently addresses the problem at hand. The following are technologies you could consider for your business. There are different levels of automation; the software you choose depends on your business needs.

- **Limited automation:** Rule-based software partially automates these tasks.
- **Advanced automation:** Rule-based software robots (Robotic Process Automation) automate repeatable, manual tasks that users perform when interacting with software.
- **Limited autonomy:** Machine learning-based software automates repeatable steps based on patterns in the underlying data.

- **Advanced autonomy:** Generative AI-based agents execute tasks on behalf of a user based on a defined objective. We cover AI agents in the section "Examining Emerging Agent-Based Systems" in chapter ten.

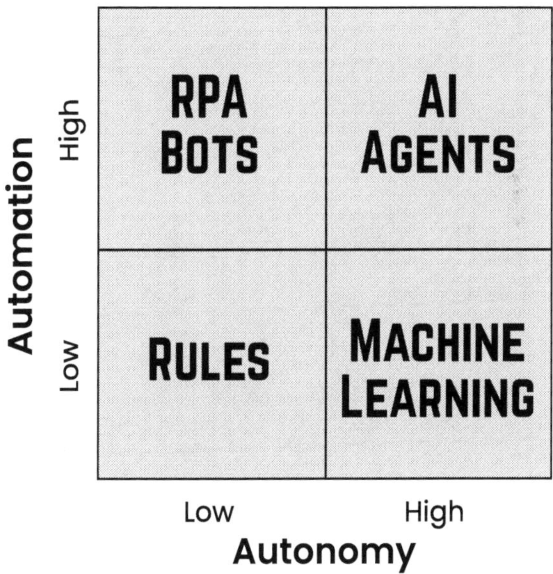

Automation and Autonomy Levels

There is no shame in using a technology other than AI to solve a business problem. There is a growing misconception by business leaders that Generative is a panacea. But even if the team can solve the business problem with AI, Generative AI won't be the method to solve all of them. It might be updating rules or automating a step with a software robot without involving any AI capabilities. For example, Generative AI generates text, images, video, or audio content. However, the current models need further enhancement regarding math and factual accuracy. Hence, Generative AI is not the best-suited technology for generating statistical results such as the ones used in demand forecasts. But you could use it to describe observed trends in a more extended report, something it could easily do once you feed it the data from your demand forecast.

Here are some other examples of when it's best to use Machine Learning.

Technology	Method	Examples
Machine Learning	Regression	Demand forecasting
	Classification	Document categories Images
	Recommendation	Products Movies
	Clustering	Customer groups Fraud detection
Generative AI	Generation	Code Blog posts Stock images Synthetic voices Talking head videos
	Summarization	Meeting transcripts Contracts
	Assistance	Writing assistants Style checkers
	Translation	Videos Chats

Artificial Intelligence Techniques

Once you have implemented your chosen AI strategy, the next step is operationalizing it. To do that well, you must build a strong AI culture within your organization. We will cover how you can achieve this in chapter 5.

In the next chapter, we discuss the multi-disciplinary field beyond data and technology in which AI leaders operate. From the emerging role of the Chief AI Officer to guiding business transformation and managing stakeholder expectations, leaders need to prepare for a demanding environment riddled with conflicting priorities.

Key Takeaways

Even the most promising technologies, such as AI, must be aligned with the business strategy to deliver tangible results. We've discussed:

- Despite AI's hype, basic management theory principles also apply to AI. For AI to support a business effectively, the technology must be aligned with its strategy and overarching goals.
- External events influence your business to update its business strategy. AI is one technology among several that can help you keep your business relevant.
- Leaders who fully embrace AI in their company are committed to changing the business model from the ground up and not just in pockets of innovation.
- Generative AI can assist business users across different functions. The initial wave of innovation is focused on increased productivity gains.

- Using AI for more tasks comes with a gradual transition from limited automation to advanced autonomy and an increased delegation of responsibilities to AI applications.

Further Reading

- Vashishta, Vin. 2023. *From Data to Profit: How Businesses Leverage Data to Grow Their Top and Bottom Lines.* Wiley. 978-1394196210.
- Davenport, Tom H. and Nitin Mittal. 2023. *All-In on AI: How Smart Companies Win Big with Artificial Intelligence.* Harvard Business Review. 978-1647824693.
- Gilmurray, Kieran. 2022. *The A-Z of Organizational Digital Transformation.* 979-8810494881.

Chapter Three

LEADING IN THE AI ERA

Leading AI Programs With the Chief AI Officer Role

Who leads AI programs in a business is as diverse as the nature of business itself. Unlike the roles of a Chief Information Officer (CIO) or Chief Technology Officer (CTO), until the last few years, there has not been a single role responsible for defining and executing a business's AI strategy. The specifics depend on the company's size, industry, and AI maturity. AI leaders are typically middle managers and senior executives in data and analytics, IT, or data science roles. For example, you may have a Director of AI who reports to the CTO or a Senior AI Manager who reports to the VP of IT, who reports to the CIO.

But recently, the dynamic has been shifting, and there's a new C-Level role: the *Chief AI Officer (CAIO)*. What might appear to be job title inflation brings real merit. CAIOs establish AI as a core capability of the business. Even the US federal government recognizes the need for a dedicated leader and plans to hire at least 400 CAIOs[13].

CAIOs largely spearhead four aspects across the business: (Additional details on the following points are covered in chapter five).

- **Knowledge:** They know new methods, trends, and tools. They maintain a network of AI experts through conferences and personal connections. This knowledge and insight helps them anticipate future developments and their impact on their business. It also allows them to prepare for using these technologies and techniques effectively.
- **Enablement:** They share their knowledge with the organization and stakeholders, preparing business and technology teams to leverage AI best. These teams need to collaborate closely to use AI effectively. This collaboration entails raising awareness of AI and its capabilities among business stakeholders and helping them see AI's potential for their domain.
- **Governance:** They define the structure, processes, and skills required for the business to remain competitive in

13 White House, 2023, "Proposed Memorandum for the Heads of Executive Departments and Agencies," November 2023, https://www.whitehouse.gov/wp-content/uploads/2023/11/AI-in-Government-Memo-draft-for-public-review.pdf.

AI in the future. Establishing standards and protocols is essential, especially in the early stages of AI maturity. CAIOs often lead the Center of Excellence (CoE) for AI in their business.

- **Vision:** They collaborate closely with their stakeholders to determine how AI can deliver the highest value to the business. Tight collaboration and alignment are critical for ensuring that the projects you pursue meet your business stakeholders' objectives—not just at the beginning of a project, but also throughout and upon delivery.

To have the maximum impact on the business, the CAIO should directly report to the CEO or divisional president for whom they work. This reporting line ensures that the CAIO will have sufficient insight into the business, oversight over AI topics, and the ability to collaborate as a peer with other members of the C-Suite.

Suppose they report to another C-Level, such as the Chief Data Officer (CDO) or the Chief Information Officer (CIO). Under those circumstances, the CAIO will be asked to contribute to the metrics and objectives by which the CDO or CIO units are measured—for example, the ratio of data usage vs. available data, or infrastructure capacity utilization rate. These metrics are different from tracking measurable business impact through AI. Additionally, this reporting line can severely restrict the CAIO's ability to develop and drive an innovation and transformation agenda across the business, if the business leaders view it as a technology-driven initiative due to organizational boundaries.

Oftentimes, budget constraints in the CDO/CIO units or relegating the AI team to a narrow, data-centric charter present further core challenges for the CAIO and their teams. Unless CAIOs gain more independence and autonomy, they won't be able to drive the change necessary to compete effectively in the market.

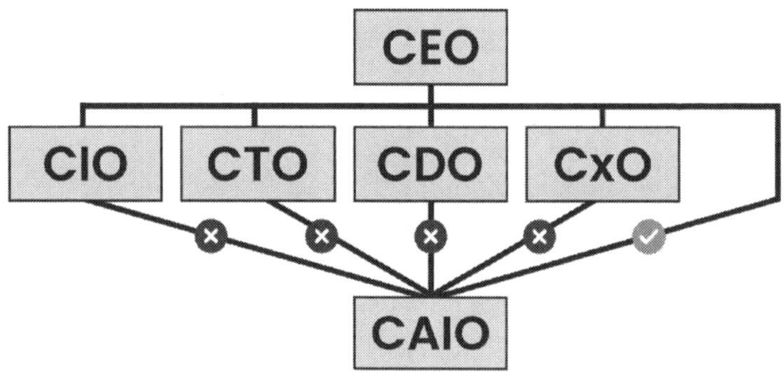

The Chief AI Officer's Reporting Line

In the past, new C-Level titles were often temporary until the technology or concept became a more widely accepted practice and the transformation was well underway or completed. The most recent example is the rise and fall of the Chief Digital Officer (CDO), whose mission has been to lead the digital transformation of a company's operations and processes. Even if the CAIO title faces a similar fate, it will evolve as AI programs become part of a business's DNA. What is certain, though, is the need for a central AI leadership role that oversees the AI initiative and can work on eye level with their peers to have a transformational impact.

If your organization does not have a dedicated CAIO role, leading AI from within another department, such as Technology or IT, can be a viable alternative if you can work with business stakeholders across the company on eye-level. You will need to ensure that your senior leaders (CEO and CxO) establish your role and team with a cross-functional mandate (authority to work with multiple stakeholders in various business functions) and that their peers in different business functions are accountable for supporting the company's AI strategy.

Additionally, your C-Level leaders should support you in case of pushback and concerns from their peers. Depending upon the size of your company, establishing a monthly review between your C-Level leader, their business peer, and you (plus the CEO if possible) can be a good rhythm to demonstrate progress and surface any challenges, roadblocks, or need for support.

Setting Realistic Goals Around Business Transformation

A common motivation for businesses to pursue AI is the greater need and aspiration to transform business operations. Whether enabling more digital processes within a company or transforming the manufacturing process of products, as an AI leader, you play a pivotal role in this process. But not every project has to be about transformation. Businesses can also go through reformations and improve existing operations with the help of AI. The difference between transformation and reformation lies in the nature of change itself. Transformation seeks to take the current state as the baseline and improve it by changing its structure. Reformation, on the other hand, aims to change a process or product while keeping its structure intact. AI plays an important role in enabling this change. Your role is to manage expectations toward your executives and convey the opportunities and limitations of the technology.

The more senior a leader is in the organization, the further away they often are from daily operations and technology. Hence, a common misconception you will encounter when working with your senior executives is that Generative AI is a panacea for any business problem. However, that is not the case. Every technology has its strengths and weaknesses. That's why understanding a technology's individual strengths is essential in selecting the right technology. For example, Generative AI's strengths are quickly analyzing, summarizing, translating, and creating new information. But, despite the current excitement about Generative AI and its ability to work extremely well on text, this technology won't reliably predict your demand forecast or optimize your field service route, which are based on mathematical operations and optimization. However, these are precisely Machine Learning's strengths, emphasizing the need for a solid understanding of the technologies and when to use which one. The more precise you can communicate and manage expectations with senior leadership, the higher your chances for success. However, managing expectations goes beyond explaining the capabilities and limitations of the technology itself.

Senior leaders want to know what results they can expect and by when. These results could be individual AI features the AI team plans on delivering or even specific business results these features will enable and how AI will improve them. Creating a roadmap of items will help AI leaders provide transparency and have a document for communicating with their leadership and stakeholders across the organization. The question is: *What can you achieve when using milestones to measure your team's progress?*

When conceiving ideas for new AI products, it is easy to get stuck or to end up with "small potato" use cases. These use cases might solve a specific problem. Still, they are much more limited in scope and impact than big transformational ideas that challenge the status quo or create new market realities. Business stakeholders frequently don't know what big-picture capabilities AI could enable. That's why when people in the organization submit ideas for new AI use cases, they often look at opportunities within their immediate scope of work. To identify transformational opportunities that can move the business forward, AI team members must understand the broader vision and ambition of the business and work their way backward.

Traditionally, companies have been cautious in introducing innovation into their operations. For the past seven to eight years, AI has often been a point solution for niche use cases. Businesses' risk aversion has led to introducing small workflow changes rather than completely overhauling their operations. But given the overall investment and organizational change management required to maximize AI's potential in a business, introducing AI must demonstrate a measurable return on investment (ROI). Without it, it is just another solution looking for a problem. Too often, teams choose aspired outcomes such as "happier employees" or "fewer clicks" without hard business metrics. The former are indeed aspirational, but they are also much harder to justify and prove than an AI product's impact on reducing the time to create a sales quote or to approve a purchase order.

You are the champion of your team's projects and must market their accomplishments. If you have a rather technical background and are more introverted than extroverted, marketing your team can feel uncomfortable to you. Remember: If you're not going to do it, nobody else will do it on your behalf. If nobody in the business knows about your team and whom you've recently helped or what impact your team has had, you will quickly see the effect: less impactful use cases or even a dried-up idea pipeline. But that doesn't have to be your fate. You will want to look for opportunities and individuals who can help you scale without working on every piece along the way. Several successful AI leaders have built multiplier communities across their businesses. These multipliers are advocates for your organization and for how your organization can support the business. But where can you find these multipliers? Starting with early adopters within a business unit is often a fruitful approach. *Who is an innovator? Who has much influence within that business area?*

You might choose a more formal or informal approach depending on your company's size. In large organizations, identifying early adopters is often a top-down approach. You pitch the idea to your peers or get buy-in from the CEO or President to nominate individuals in their business units. In smaller organizations, you will often know the colleagues who have an affinity for new technologies. They are the ones who, independent of their role, love tinkering with robotics, Internet of Things devices, or home automation, participating in RoboCup events or adding sensors to bee hives to measure the amount of honey from afar. This curiosity and interest in learning about new capabilities is important as these colleagues constantly look for opportunities to apply technology. They are also the ones who see problems and have ideas on how to solve them. Often, these early adopters are in senior-level to first-level leadership roles close to the daily business operations and already have sufficient understanding of the business and a good reputation within their business units and teams.

Learn about their role and their team's goals. What are their key performance indicators (KPIs)? How could AI help them reach their business goals? Try to approach them with a proposal on how your team can support them. Ensure you use your stakeholders' language—not tech jargon. Keeping your stakeholders engaged and informed is vital; not just at the beginning or end of a project, but throughout. This alignment helps ensure they know the progress and can comment on any deviations impacting the project's next steps. It also allows business and technology stakeholders to determine if the project should continue.

Engaging your stakeholders throughout the process is one of the most critical aspects of leadership in developing new technologies. Depending upon your company, culture, and stakeholders' preference to consume information, this could range from sending a status report to a formal meeting.

Using Storytelling to Get Stakeholder Buy-In

AI leaders often make a crucial mistake when meeting their stakeholders—one that costs time and personal credibility. They spend most of the meeting talking about technical terms. They frequently need more time to discuss the next steps, and their stakeholders need more patience to tolerate the jargon. In addition to business acumen and technical understanding, storytelling is an equally essential tool in your repertoire. When applied effectively, you can get buy-in for a project the company should pursue, acquire additional resources to work on other projects, or get funding to do the above.

But not everyone is comfortable with storytelling. Many technology leaders perceive storytelling as inauthentic or lacking depth. They start by telling the steps they have taken to reach the conclusion rather than highlighting the outcomes first and, only if requested, sharing more details about the journey. After all, until your stakeholders understand why your story and project are important to them, they will not be receptive to listening about the steps that have gotten you there.

When sharing details about a project, many leaders follow a classic five-act story framework. You may not have realized it, but from an early age, we are trained to structure and process stories along this very framework. Whether it is in school or college, these techniques were likely refined and rewarded until you entered the business world. However, there is one key concept in this framework that most business leaders miss when presenting information to their peers and executives: conveying the business outcome executives can expect. Without that, your story most likely goes something like this:

Act	General Concept	Classic AI Story
Exposition	Main characters and backstory	High-level overview of the business challenge
Rising Action	Conflict arises	Problem statement and setting the stage for the solution
Climax	Peak of tension or turning point	Methodology and discoveries
Falling Action	Action towards resolution	Next steps and implementation strategies
Resolution	Tragic or happy end	Summary and a call to action

Classic Five-Act Story Framework

"Today, I'll present the status of our AI project to improve customer retention. We observed that customer churn increased by 20% last quarter. We pulled data from our CRM system and social media data and applied logistic regression. As you can see in the confusion matrix, the true-positive and true-negative values are very high. The model has a confidence score of 0.91. Also, a precision of 0.96 and recall of 0.69."

That's the point in the story arc where technical leaders lose the attention of their business stakeholders, who are likely unfamiliar with data science metrics and their meaning. Without noticing that their attention has dropped, you continue your talk track. (It has happened to me before as well.)

"The model's f1-score of 0.83 shows a high reliability of the model's predictions. We did some more feature engineering [...]. Ultimately, we found that first-time orders and negative sentiment online about the delivery times within three weeks of the purchase date indicate the highest influencing factors for customer churn..."

With only a few minutes left in your slot on the agenda, you are effectively running out of time to discuss the next steps and recommended decisions. You missed an opportunity to demonstrate the impact of your team and AI product on business.

So, what is the problem with this five-act framework we learned in school? It comes down to the goal of effective storytelling in business: capturing your stakeholders' attention and getting to a decision—not evoking emotions or diving into the intricate details of the main protagonists' backgrounds.

The story should, therefore, include facts and numbers to support your main points. But even beyond that, many data and AI leaders still underestimate a critical point: The story you tell needs to convey what business outcome your stakeholders can expect if they act upon your recommendation—and how the results of your AI project support the business strategy. For example, remember to show how quarterly deliverables help your business reach its long-term ambitions with AI.

So, how should you structure your story when presenting it to your stakeholders? Instead of the classic five-act story arc, structure your story along the *AIDA framework* (Attention, Interest, Desire, Action) for stakeholder meetings.

Phase	General Concept	AIDA AI Story
Attention	Get your stakeholders' awareness on the subject	Compelling fact or question
Interest	Develop their interest in the topic	Importance of topic
Desire	Nurture their willingness to get its benefits	Demonstrate solutions and benefits
Action	Make it simple for your stakeholders to approve or move forward	Immediate action

AIDA Framework for Business Storytelling

Following the AIDA framework, you will captivate your audience: *"Last quarter, we lost two customers for every ten that have our product. As a result, our customer acquisition cost has increased from $34 to $59. But the reason behind this customer churn is not what you would expect."*

Aren't you curious as well, at this point, about how the story continues?

"We found that first-time orders and negative sentiment online about the delivery times within three weeks of the purchase date have the highest impact on customer churn. We recommend reviewing the operations of our third-party logistics provider [...] to remediate this situation immediately and reduce our customer acquisition cost and churn again."

This framework allows you to raise and maintain your audience's attention from the beginning of your presentation while quickly presenting actionable decision alternatives. You can use the time with your business stakeholders to discuss options that move the business forward based on your team's impact instead of diving into the details of how you have arrived at the recommendation.

In addition to applying a framework such as AIDA, practice makes perfect. Practice your talk track and delivery several dozen times before you deliver it to your stakeholders. These changes will help keep your audience's attention and focus on conveying what's in it for them.

You can even ask your business stakeholders to present to your senior leadership about the AI products you have built together instead of doing it yourself. They can share in the terms of their business function what value the AI capabilities you have developed together create for your customers or operations. Proof of value from leaders other than yourself adds legitimacy to your claim that AI improves the business. The more your peers can contextualize AI in their work and demonstrate that it does deliver a business impact, the more valuable your team becomes for the business, and the stronger the support from the top will be to create more impactful AI products.

AI leaders and their stakeholders often view AI as a project. However, this approach frequently leads to issues that we will discuss in the next chapter.

Key Takeaways

Now that the AI strategy to support the business strategy is defined, it's time to discuss how to implement it:

- The Chief AI Officer (CAIO) is a new role in the C-Suite. The role encompasses educating and enabling the organization on AI, establishing guidelines and best practices, and advocating among their peers.
- CAIOs can be most effective when reporting directly to the president of a division they are responsible for or the company's CEO. In smaller companies, a reporting relationship within Technology or IT can be successful as well if you have sufficient support from the top.
- Whether or not your business already has a CAIO, stakeholder management is critical to leading AI. Your leadership's expectations of the AI program are

high. As an AI leader, it's your role to manage these expectations realistically while delivering on the vision.

- AI programs aim to transform businesses for a new era, make them more competitive, and create more value for customers. However, reforming instead of transforming a process can bring sufficient change.
- You must hone your storytelling to get buy-in and support for implementing changes. Unlike the traditional story arc we learn in school, you must get to the point quickly and provide insight into what's in it for your audience.

Further Reading

- Evergreen, Brian. 2023. *Autonomous Transformation: Creating a More Human Future in the Era of Artificial Intelligence*. Wiley. 978-1119985297.
- Taylor, Scott. 2020. *Telling Your Data Story: Data Storytelling for Data Management*. Technics Publications. 978-1634628952.

Part II:

ENABLING ORGANIZATIONAL SUCCESS

Strategy and leadership are the foundation; however, leading AI programs in business needs to go further. When stakeholders collaborate across the business and understand AI's benefits, they see opportunities previously hidden in plain sight. They can shape an innovation culture that embraces technological advancement. But adoption does not happen overnight. Projects often fall short of expectations as they are short-term rather than long-term oriented. Leaders can enable AI success by pivoting toward a product mindset for AI.

Chapter Four

DESIGNING FOR PEOPLE

Distinguishing Between Projects and Products

The most common approach in business to doing something new and timely is creating a project for it. This approach has been ingrained in modern organizations and is the method of choice for anything from minor changes to significant transformations. Therefore, it is logical that leaders new to AI approach it like introducing any other organizational change—as a project. However, as it turns out, this is the biggest mistake new leaders make early on, and the approach you choose will set the trajectory of the entire AI endeavor.

AI projects are unlike any other data or IT projects. You need to translate business problems into an abstraction based on data and deal with approximations as results as opposed to absolute answers. AI projects are much more akin to research projects that include experimentation rather than linear projects in which the feasibility of the outcome is typically known at the start. That is why there is a growing perception to pivot from AI *projects* toward *products*. The main differences become clear along five dimensions: the leader's role, the audience, the tool to steer the effort, the mindset, and the next steps in the endeavor.

Dimension	AI Project	AI Product
Leader	Project manager	Product owner
Audience	Stakeholders	Users
Tool	Project plan	User stories
Mindset	Discrete event	Continuous evolution
Next step	New project	Roadmap items

Comparison of AI Projects and AI Products

The Project Manager vs. Product Manager/Owner

Project managers typically lead an AI project. They work with key stakeholders across the organization to ensure alignment and to make progress. They use a project plan that includes deliverables, timelines, and responsible project members. This project plan helps the team understand their current position on the journey to completion, the work ahead of them, and whether they expect to complete the project on time. Projects are discrete initiatives that have an end date. Once the project is completed, any changes or enhancements to the delivered outcome will likely initiate a new project.

Products are fundamentally different and, therefore, require a different mindset that is new for data and IT teams used to working on projects: Instead of a project manager, the *product owner* defines the product's shape and assigns the team and jobs to be done. Applying a product mindset ensures that the user is at the center of the AI initiative and that their needs are already incorporated in the design and development of the AI product. A great way to do this is creating a persona of your target user. This persona includes gender, age, profession, wants and needs, as well as typical business problems that they face. For example:

> *Mary is a 42-year old accounting manager in a large enterprise. She is married and has two teenage children, Dan and Jane. At work, she enjoys working with her team to optimize treasury for the company. But inefficient planning and forecasting make it difficult for her and the team to achieve optimal results. She would like to use more insights and automation, but is rather skeptical of it when systems provide limited context of how they have arrived at a recommendation. Mary is influential within the company's finance department. Winning her support can open doors to other finance leaders.*

In combination with user stories, these methods describe the end-users' experience with the AI product. Thereby, it is clear from the very beginning for whom the team develops this AI product and what characteristics to pay special attention to. Unlike AI projects, AI products continuously evolve and improve based on a defined roadmap. *What feedback do our users and customers give us? Which features should we develop first? What are the next set of features that our users are asking for? How could we increase our revenue for this product?* However, it can take several projects to deliver and grow a product. By applying a product mindset, the AI team can take a long-term view for the product strategy while delivering on short-term deliverables in a project fashion.

Contrary to one-time projects, products also allow the AI team to think about monetizing AI in three steps: *productize, commercialize, and monetize.* During the productization phase, the team decides how to package the AI models and features so customers can easily consume them. Commercialization looks at taking the AI product and defining the best channels to sell and operate it, including via an ecosystem of partners. The third step, monetization, spans terms and conditions, sales contracts, and the actual pricing of the AI product. By adopting a product mindset, organizations focus on delivering outcomes, such as increased customer value.

Recognizing Inhibitors to AI Project Success and Adoption

AI projects fail despite the best efforts to create a model, validate it, and move it into production. In 2018, Gartner estimated that approx 85% of AI projects fail *to deliver the expected value*[14] (often misinterpreted as the *percentage of projects that fail*). Based on a 2022 survey by Gartner[15], only about 54% of AI projects moved from pilot into production. That is marginally better than flipping a coin to determine the success of an AI project. In 2024, Gartner[16] reported that approximately 30% of all Generative AI projects in 2024 do not progress past the proof-of-concept stage.

The reason for project failures is rarely bad intentions but rather missing a clearly defined business problem and a thorough assessment of whether AI can solve this problem to begin with. Even *if* AI can solve this particular business problem, you will need to find out if the required data is available and if you can access it. However, analyzing whether data is available is often overlooked. In some cases, if the data is not available, you will

---

14 Gartner, 2018, "Gartner Says Nearly Half of CIOs Are Planning to Deploy Artificial Intelligence," February 13, 2018, https://www.gartner.com/en/newsroom/press-releases/2018-02-13-gartner-says-nearly-half-of-cios-are-planning-to-deploy-artificial-intelligence.

15 Gartner, 2022, "Gartner Survey Reveals 80% of Executives Think Automation Can Be Applied to Any Business Decision," August 22, 2022, https://www.gartner.com/en/newsroom/press-releases/2022-08-22-gartner-survey-reveals-80-percent-of-executives-think-automation-can-be-applied-to-any-business-decision.

16 Gartner, 2024, "Gartner Predicts 30% of Generative AI Projects Will Be Abandoned After Proof of Concept By End of 2025," July 29, 2024, https://www.gartner.com/en/newsroom/press-releases/2024-07-29-gartner-predicts-30-percent-of-generative-ai-projects-will-be-abandoned-after-proof-of-concept-by-end-of-2025.

need to wait until sufficient transactional data has been created through actual business transactions.

Most AI projects originate in technology-focused departments like IT, data, or AI. This setup frequently leads to AI teams building products in an echo chamber, without proper input of domain experts in the business. By combining technical and business experts on diverse, cross-functional teams, they can prioritize the AI features that are expected to create the highest business benefit and solve a tangible problem that the business function faces. Without bringing these two stakeholder groups together, technology-focused teams can have a tendency to prioritize the most sophisticated solution and newest technology, instead of features based on their usefulness for their business stakeholders. Lastly, the most promising AI product validated by the most diverse team will only see adoption if you can also implement it.

Change management is a critical aspect that can accelerate adoption of your AI product across the business. But often, skepticism among end-users about AI-generated insights and recommendations as well as users' overreliance on their gut feeling based on years of first-hand experience are underestimated. As a result, users are more opposed to using AI and trusting its predictions, and they circumvent or override what the AI product has generated or predicted. This will often lead to suboptimal results as humans have fewer data points available to analyze, and emotions influence our decisions.

But even when following the best change management practices, the adoption of your AI product might fail. A lot of times, business leaders want to get the new AI product into the hands of their domain experts quickly. After all, time is money. However, when leaders push to follow that approach, they often try to do too much. Instead of rolling out the new AI product in one go, experiment with piloting a semi-finished product in a limited market and keep improving it. This iterative process can balance speed and relevance while minimizing the margin for wide-scale error. But even if you do follow a phased approach, ensure that you don't roll out any unproven, biased models by deploying too soon. Building AI products is more akin to research and experimentation than a start-to-finish project, and it can frequently lead to longer timelines to complete the delivery of an AI feature. If this timeline keeps getting pushed out, the omnipresent organizational change will further slow your progress. For example, company or business priorities might change throughout your AI project: Your business sponsor may move to a different unit or leave the company, or the budget earmarked to support your project could be needed to fund other initiatives that deliver higher value and return more quickly.

Organizations and their leaders who have been on an AI journey for several years have also developed an understanding of what AI can do for them and where its limitations lie. A significant shift in expectations is leaders' awareness that AI is probabilistic, not deterministic. AI is an approximation, not an absolute, failure-proof guarantee for accurate, repeatable results.

But, these challenges do not only affect AI products that support a business's internal processes. Even consumer-facing products are not immune to a lack of adoption and inadequate use. While chatbots and voice input were key capabilities of previous generations of AI, they have struggled to live up to expectations. Amazon Alexa is an excellent example of this situation. When Amazon introduced the voice assistant in 2014, the company envisioned its customers interacting with the device to order and reorder products from its e-commerce store. However, it turned out that its users would use Alexa as an interface to control their smart home devices, ask for the time and weather, or have the voice assistant read the news[17]. As a result, the revenue which Alexa was expected to generate has remained below expectations. Hence, any AI product must include constant user research.

For example, capturing the initial prompts that new users submit (while following rules and regulations) could provide a better understanding of *how* they use your product. From there, your teams can derive how to improve the UX to make your AI product more intuitive for new users.

---

17 Ars Technica, 2022, "Amazon Alexa Is A 'Colossal Failure,' On Pace To Loose $10 Billion This Year," November 21, 2022. https://arstechnica.com/gadgets/2022/11/amazon-alexa-is-a-colossal-failure-on-pace-to-lose-10-billion-this-year/.

Enabling Product Teams on AI

Product teams are uniquely positioned at the intersection of technology, application, and users to identify and validate opportunities. Product managers might be wondering about the impact of AI on their jobs. Oftentimes, they are just as concerned about the increased use of AI in their roles as business teams are.

Given the uncertainty of the situation, these fears are only human. Therefore, it is vital that you communicate clearly and transparently your motivations and aspirations for introducing AI in the business. The more precise you are, the better your chances of alleviating these concerns. However, communicating alone will not suffice. Your words need to be congruent with your actions.

You can lead the way and help product teams understand the new opportunities that AI provides to create personas and user journeys and organize product roadmaps. Product managers can leverage and learn from the abundant information available on the internet, such as formal training, communities, podcasts, and conferences. These resources help individuals stay up-to-date on industry best practices and extend their network with peers who might be further ahead on their AI journey. Suppose team members in your organization are worried about the impact of AI on their jobs. In that case, you can organize sessions and events within your business as another valuable source of information and actively shape the conversation about the use of AI in your organization toward AI-enabled product management.

In addition to using AI to increase efficiency, product managers must also understand the cost structure of adding an AI feature to a product. In the case of Generative AI, that includes suppliers' pricing, the number of input and output tokens, and the expected number of transactions per month or year. (We will talk more about tokens in Ensuring Relevant Output in chapter 8.) Consider whether the feature should be built using off-the-shelf components (generic), by augmenting readily available APIs (company-specific data), or by fine-tuning or maybe even creating a model from scratch (proprietary, competitive advantage)—and even whether to build it in the first place. Before deciding which feature to pursue, user research and understanding customers' willingness to pay are essential input factors for making a decision. After all, Generative AI incurs additional costs.

	Included	**Per user**	**Transactional**
Pros	Simple for customer	Simple for customer Average out spikes	Accurate billing Harder to trace
Cons	Risk of cost for overconsumption	Risk of overconsumption	Complexity for customer

Comparison of Pricing Approaches

Whether the planned feature is used in a company-internal application or as part of a commercially available product, understanding usage patterns helps estimate and anticipate costs.

But it is not just about managing product- and cost-related aspects, and bringing your product teams along on the AI journey. You need to go further and embrace AI-driven change in your entire business by shaping an innovation culture. In the next chapter, we discuss how you can get started.

Key Takeaways

In this chapter, we've learned:

- Although AI is often approached as a project, there's a growing shift toward viewing it with a product mindset. Unlike projects, products put the end-user at the center of the focus (not the end date) and deliver according to a roadmap (not a project plan).
- Developing AI products is more akin to conducting research than well-established IT projects. AI leaders need to balance the uncertainty of the outcome with making progress on the immediate deliverables.
- Despite the best intentions, AI initiatives (regardless of being approached as projects or products) can fail. The main reasons for a lack of AI adoption are unclear value proposition, stakeholder engagement, and poor change management.
- Business users are not the only ones concerned about the increased use of AI. Product teams might also be worried that AI will take over more of their jobs. Your role is to manage this conversation.

- Product teams must understand their suppliers' pricing models and estimate the fixed and transactional costs for incorporating AI into their applications. Depending upon the vendor and product, three approaches have emerged for AI: included in the main application, per user, and transactional pricing.

Chapter Five

CULTIVATING AN AI-READY CULTURE

Raising AI Fluency Across the Organization

A leader's aspiration to implement AI across the business needs to encompass more than connecting AI to the business strategy. It requires a cultural change and AI-literate team members throughout the organization. There is so much hype around AI and so many buzzwords flying around that you must be fluent in the terminology *and* its meaning. Given AI's potential impact on a business (good or bad), creating AI fluency within the organization is crucial. An organization can increase AI fluency in two directions: within the leadership team (horizontally) and among employees (vertically).

Learning about AI is challenging, given dozens of competing business priorities. However, to identify AI opportunities and understand the order of magnitude with which AI will transform businesses and industries, so-called *AI fluency* is a new critical skill for any leader in this era, as is having an understanding of finance or sales processes. After all, if you don't understand the technology, how can you expect your teams to do so, and how can you effectively move the business forward into this new era (or guide it through rough waters if the competition takes the lead first) if you can neither see the opportunities nor the threats?

Luckily, Generative AI is making the technology more accessible than previous generations of AI. Anyone can use tools like ChatGPT without prior knowledge of core data science and building models. Many Generative AI tools are even available at your fingertips, on your smartphone—anytime and anywhere. This ease of access makes the technology much more accessible to experiment with and grasp. C-Level leaders and executives can experience AI much more immediately than ever before. Instead of delving into the intricacies of complex, domain-specific statistical models for fraud detection in financial services, leaders can interact with AI-enabled tools from their browsers. For them, developing AI fluency means understanding AI's conceptual capabilities. They can now ask themselves, *What can AI do and not do? How does AI fit into our business strategy?* This knowledge will help leaders prioritize and pursue the most promising AI use cases that contribute to their business strategy and goals. However, it is not only leaders who need to develop AI fluency. Generative AI makes benefitting from the latest technology built into applications easier.

For example, team members can now interact with software as if they were having a conversation with another person. It is akin to bouncing ideas off a colleague or coaching a junior team member. That further lowers the entry barrier. No lengthy or formal training programs are needed. But, providing opportunities for employees to use tools such as ChatGPT and the like is important for getting them acquainted with new technologies and for learning how to use these tools in their work. Because, for example, searching for information using Generative AI tools differs from a Google search query. It is more conversational and iterative. It takes some unlearning, but getting into that new rhythm is the first step.

Across the entire organization, employees need to learn about AI. They need to understand how to leverage AI, how to work alongside it, how their role will evolve, and how to spot its limitations. A practical method for facilitating this upskilling is building education and multiplier programs. As an AI leader, you don't need to do that alone; you should provide sufficient input to connect business and technology aspects. Depending upon the size of your business, you can either collaborate with your HR learning and development team or involve a vendor specializing in AI literacy training.

Start creating AI and Generative AI fluency by working with senior leaders such as a Chief Human Resources Officer,

Chief Revenue Officer, or someone in a similar role. Helping them understand the potential and seeing the opportunity first-hand creates a multiplier effect. You need this top-down support to develop and roll out effective upskilling programs. Ideally, this program is a company-wide initiative, not just in an organizational silo. Providing this enablement at scale goes with a paradigm shift of looking at AI and productivity and creating a new mindset in your organization around using AI as part of every business function. Not every C-Level leader might be receptive to increased AI use. They might be concerned about risks such as data privacy and bias as barriers to making these tools available to their workforce. It's best to address potential risks like these upfront. See chapter 9: Mitigating Potential Threats for additional details.

For your AI projects to succeed, you must help your business become more familiar with AI. This approach will help them get more comfortable with the technology, learn about its limitations, and also see its potential in the context of their work. Showing genuine curiosity and empathy for team members going through this evolution is critical for building credibility within the organization. When exploring Generative AI, approach it in three phases:

1. Deploy Generative AI for individual productivity.

Business users can learn to use these new tools in a dedicated space without leaking confidential information.

a. **Encourage safe exploration:** Create a safe space for employees to explore Generative AI without revealing sensitive data.

b. **Define acceptable use policies:** Define what your team members should use Generative AI for in your business, the type of data they should use, and which tools are recommended or permitted.
c. **Communication strategy:** Provide a safe exploration space and policies.
d. **Education:** Show how to use these tools.
e. **Incentives:** Set up a recognition program for exceptional use cases.

2. Leverage AI to increase team productivity.

Next, you can leverage your Center of Excellence (CoE) and get entire teams to buy into your AI vision and to look for opportunities in a team's operations, for example personalizing promotional emails to customers. (We will go into more detail about how you can set this up in the next chapter.) Ensure that the entire team will use the AI feature to increase productivity and provide space for them to exchange information and best practices, so they can learn from each other. Because multiple people who have varying degrees of openness to change need to adopt the AI feature at the same time, team-wide AI adoption is much harder to accomplish than individual productivity scenarios.

3. Define moonshots to move into new markets.

Lastly, by defining a few moonshots (highly visionary and ambitious projects that challenge the status quo), you can counter strategy decay and capitalize on transformational opportunities to move into new markets or offer new products and services.

While encouraging business users to use Generative AI tools is only the first step toward increased productivity over time, you will need to provide guidelines along with this encouragement. The most relevant one is applying the *Socratic method.* Generative AI can be a helpful assistant, but users should not trust it unquestioningly. It is the equivalent of asking a stranger on the street for information and taking it as gospel. Business users should validate the generated output by asking follow-up questions and independently verifying the information. Generative AI tools can boost creativity and productivity, however, they are not a substitute for independent, critical thinking.

Traditionally, technology and business teams need to communicate better. One talks about technological capabilities, while the other is looking to improve their business outcomes with the help of technology. This gap frequently leads to misaligned understandings of projects, scope, and requirements. But leaders like you play a central role in driving change. You have an opportunity to lead by example. As a technology-focused leader, you need to learn about the business before you can become even more effective in coaching your team members. When you do, it's essential that you look beyond the technical aspects that help evaluate a model and focus on business requirements, KPIs, and measurable outcomes as well.

ChatGPT and the like are just some of the tools that business users should become familiar with. Raising awareness of the fundamental concepts of data and how data is the foundation for predictions and decisions is essential to conceiving higher-level opportunities. It includes understanding:

1. How organizations capture data about individuals
2. How organizations use analytics to uncover patterns in consumer behavior
3. How statistics and probabilities inform business decisions

Building upon that foundational understanding, you can explore together with your business stakeholders how your business can improve these probabilities to create more economic value and how to measure value in the first place. Maximizing value must incorporate ethics, as our behavior and biases manifest in the captured data. Fostering an inclusive culture is equally part of creating AI literacy. Users have a responsibility akin to citizens: being informed, proactive, and interested in how others use their data.

Introducing any AI-enabled product in the organization eventually changes how people work. There is a high degree of uncertainty because of the hype in the media and industries and the uncertainty of AI's impact on the business down to someone's role. As a leader, instilling trust is a core aspect of your responsibility. Whether team members trust the leadership's intentions to augment rather than replace people, or team members trust the predictions and the output that AI products generate, trust is a critical factor for using AI products adequately. However, when uncertainty or expectations are high, the risk of incorrect use of AI is also high. That is why building trust in AI across the organization requires several factors to be considered. Among the first factors is the impact on individuals' jobs and the perceived impact by the individuals. There are three different mindsets with which individuals approach the increased availability of AI in business:

- **Job protectionism:** The jobs of the present must remain unchanged.
- **Job fatalism:** Machines will take over our jobs.
- **Job pragmatism:** Change is coming, and we need to prepare for it.

You will experience all three mindsets when you talk to employees across the company. Given the pace of innovation, individuals who have adopted a *job pragmatism* view will be best prepared to leverage new technologies and adapt to change. They see the changes and embrace them. These individuals are prime candidates to become part of your multiplier community. More on that in chapter 6: Improving Communication Between Technical and Business Teams. *Job protectionism* argues for the status quo to continue. You can address these concerns by referring to examples of rapid advancements in AI technology and the business's need to remain competitive. Both aspects combined make retaining the status quo often infeasible in the long run, especially if competitors embrace change more quickly. Lastly, you need to quickly address a *job fatalism* view or prevent it from forming in the organization. Employees who have adopted this view fear that AI is going to replace their jobs. You can address their concerns by showing tangible examples of the tasks of a given role AI is able to support and where the gaps are. This education can instill a sense of realism.

Communicate with your teams clearly and directly. And do so upfront so they understand the context and can ask questions. Piloting AI in isolation in one area of the business can have a negative spill-over effect if adjacent teams feel excluded and potentially threatened by the AI. In addition to sharing what you will do and why, be clear on what you will not do. Even if your goal is to drive cost savings, you must have your team members aware and on board. If you don't, the consequence could be them undermining your efforts or negative beliefs forming about the business that will be hard to undo.

Another aspect of building trust is ensuring users trust the AI product's predictions and generated output. The explainability of predictions and results is a critical aspect of that. Vendors of Generative AI applications such as OpenAI, Google, and Microsoft have been adding disclaimers in their products that the output is generated with the help of AI and that users should double-check the results before making decisions based on them or taking action. However, these vendors now transfer the responsibility for the accuracy of their software's results to the user. Before vendors started integrating Generative AI into their products, disclaimers like this would have been unheard of. Users expect their applications to work without question, especially in a business environment where decisions lead to legal and financial implications.

Where results are based on ML-generated predictions (instead of Generative AI), model interpretation techniques such as Local Interpretable Model-agnostic Explanations (LIME) and SHapley Additive exPlanations (SHAP) can provide additional context on a model's top influencing factors (features) contributing to the final prediction. For example, software provider Intuit provides model explanations in its TurboTax software. These explanations help users understand whether their tax report is at a higher risk of being audited by tax authorities and which factors impact that prediction most. Users receive critical information upfront by highlighting factors such as high expenses in categories that are uncommon among taxpayers with similar characteristics. Based on these insights, users can then review and correct their tax report before submitting it, reducing the likelihood of being audited.

But it is not just about building trust in AI among end-users and ensuring they understand AI-generated predictions. Team members working on AI projects need a blend of related skills as well, from data preparation and data engineering to data science and prompting LLMs. They must approach AI with a product mindset, looking for opportunities to enable new business value through AI. Your team composition might vary depending on your organization's setup and charter. But generally, your AI team should comprise data engineers, data scientists, NLP experts, software developers, and business analysts. New data science team members should shadow more experienced peers on a few projects to learn about the typical questions, interactions, and priorities when working with business stakeholders. Currently, all roles will need some experience with prompt engineering—whether for data analysis, generating output, or coding. Lastly, your team must understand how to build Retrieval-Augmented Generation-based applications—more on that in the section titled "Methods for Generating More Relevant Output" in chapter 8.

Despite Generative AI lowering the barrier of entry to develop AI products, data science is still a highly important skill as businesses continue to build their own models. Technology experts are often so focused on their domain and the details of tools and approaches that optimizing the results for the highest possible degree of accuracy can quickly take precedence over practicality. The former is often the case in deeply research-driven environments. But the goal of data science in a business context fundamentally differs from an academic or research-driven context. The model you develop needs to serve a defined business purpose and deliver a return. This return could be increasing revenue or reducing costs. However, building and optimizing the model itself already comes at a price. So, optimizing it beyond a reasonable point means investing budget and resources on a task that does not create a proportional return. Understanding when the model delivers good enough results is critical to determining when to stop optimizing and putting it into production.

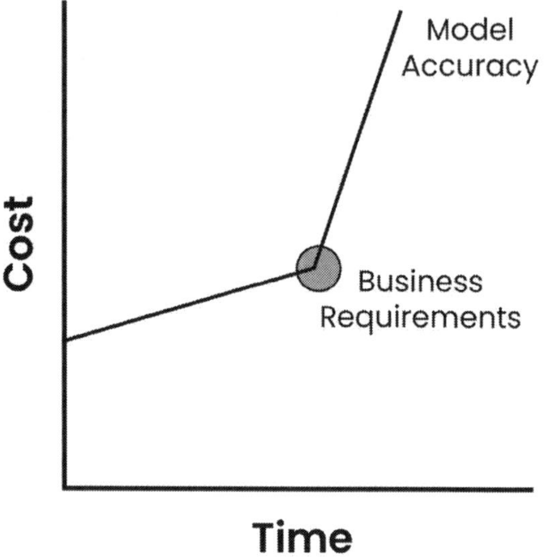

Point of Decreasing Utility

A critical aspect of determining when to stop optimizing the model is having a baseline and an expectation. Leaders unfamiliar with the domain can tend to strive for impact in the high 90th percentile. Experienced leaders and subject matter experts know that, depending on the situation, even a single-digit improvement can yield a significant return in absolute terms. The investment in improving pays for itself, especially when the improvement compounds over time.

Along with opportunities goes the question of unintended consequences and risk. You must assume that your teams' models will lead to unintended consequences. Adopting this view allows you to assess these consequences in your unique situation and how they could be addressed or mitigated. Keep in mind that not all effects are immediate in their impact. There will likely be secondary and tertiary consequences, even if the initiative is successful. For example, the model in your company's online shop recommends products to shoppers to increase the order size by cross-selling. The model's effectiveness leads to a surge in demand in a geographic area as more customers are buying your products (first order). To meet this demand, you need to ship items from distribution centers that are further away (second order). In turn, this increases your shipping cost, delivery time, and carbon footprint (third order).

Establishing a Center of Excellence

Technologies such as AI and Generative AI are new for most businesses. As an AI leader, you know you want to do something about AI, but your teams must learn about the latest technology and you need to establish a suitable governance model with your business stakeholders. As a leader who is tasked with implementing AI in your business, you can not afford to act in isolation or out of an ivory tower. Developing and introducing any AI product ultimately also introduces a change to the way people work. First and foremost, technology must support the professionals who use it daily.

When individual teams quickly explore opportunities for using AI in their business unit or team, this leads to pockets of innovation that lack standardization and the ability to use economies of scale. This is especially relevant in large, distributed organizations. Therefore, you should look for ways to explore the potential and, at the same time, drive standardization, governance, and enablement across the organization. However, only some organizations have the knowledge, tools, and processes to do this immediately.

This is where establishing a Center of Excellence (CoE) under the CAIO or AI leader's direction can truly make an impact. It consists of team members tasked with exploring the new technology, identifying opportunities for its use, piloting it, working with stakeholders across the business, and enabling them to use it. A CoE is the tip of the spear for making an emerging technology such as AI usable for the organization. To do that effectively, they must collaborate with various subject matter experts in different business functions. These experts run the business daily and are, therefore, also much closer to the actual problems that AI can solve than the technology-focused CoE. The CoE teaches these business stakeholders how to use the technology, gets them excited about it, and is there to help business stakeholders pilot and adopt the technology early on.

Although standardization is an essential role of a CoE, this ambition should not come at the expense of your business stakeholders' excitement and willingness to collaborate. Standardization also should not become an administrative burden on your stakeholders. For example, instead of asking your stakeholders to report any use of AI to your team and seeking to create a full catalog of each and every use of AI across the business, you can let teams decide which AI-enabled tools they would like to use to do their work (e.g. Microsoft 365 Copilot or Adobe Firefly) in order to foster innovation. Focusing on ensuring that new developments happen on approved platforms and that security, frameworks, and tools remain within a defined standard (that you and your AI team set) are a good starting point to maintain a healthy balance between flexibility and control. The typical scope of a CoE includes the following tasks:

- Enablement
- Standardization
- Governance
- Prototyping
- Scaling

The role of a CoE is usually confined to a specific period until the organization reaches a higher level of maturity and becomes comfortable working with the new technology regularly. Once the technology is part of the organization's day-to-day activities, the CoE may no longer be needed. That means CoEs go through a maturity curve:

1. In many organizations, CoE teams are centralized and responsible for establishing standards, processes, and governance for using AI. Their tasks involve selecting platforms and tools the organization will adopt and defining the innovation funnel—from generating ideas to productization and ongoing maintenance.
2. Over time and with the organization's increasing maturity, the organizational model evolves into a federated model with satellites spinning up in different business functions.

3. And eventually, the CoE's role shifts from establishing a beachhead to enabling others to maintain standards and processes.

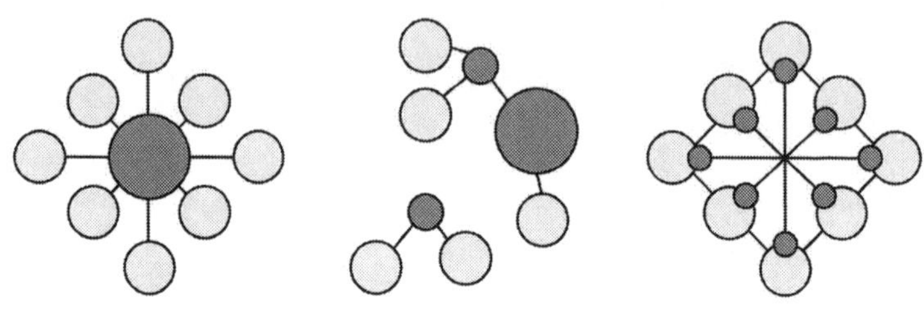

Evolution of the Center of Excellence Organizational Model

If you are going to build and lead a CoE, understanding the most common organizational structures as well as their pros and cons is critical:

- **Centralized:** This is often the initial team in the company that will be working on AI, concentrating their expertise in one central team as a Center of Excellence. The business teams provide the aspects to incorporate AI into their products and processes, such as domain expertise, technical integration, marketing, etc. *Pros:* This team can be very fast and nimble in defining the first set of standards, guidelines, and training for the wider organization, providing the speed to explore and establish a new technology topic such as AI quickly.

Cons: Depending upon the business culture, the team might face an "us vs. them" mindset and not be easily accepted by the business stakeholders. That is why close collaboration and creating an AI-ready culture are so important.

- **Federated:** Additional teams in the business are increasing their investment in AI and establishing their own CoEs, which collaborate with the central AI team. Some of your or CoE's team members will potentially move into these decentralized teams to help establish them and continue driving standardization.
  Pros: Your business is increasing its AI maturity, and your business stakeholders are investing in AI. This setup gives your team scale and experienced partners to work with within these business teams.
  Cons: Establishing AI teams in different parts of the business can lead to competition and siloed thinking. For example, these teams could decide to standardize on different technologies and platforms. Therefore, it is critical that the roles and responsibilities between your CoE and the new ones in the business are clearly defined (and as early as possible). For example, guidelines, technology, and responsible AI practices should still be centrally driven by your CoE to ensure consistency across the business. But building the innovation pipeline and vetting AI ideas can follow a process that is more tailored to the business unit the new CoEs are a part of.

- **Decentralized:** Even the last centralized AI resources are moving into business teams, evolving the collaboration further into a decentralized organizational model. This setup is the final stage of an organization's AI maturity.
  Pros: The company has fully adopted AI as a key technology. Every business team has sufficient AI expertise and resources to incorporate AI in their products and operations. Selected members from all these individual CoEs will align on evolving guidelines and using new products and technologies in a virtual team.
  Cons: Because of the distributed nature, the risk to deviate from a standard and individual teams viewing themselves as the pace-setter for innovation increases. Establishing governance and strong leadership (e.g. under the AI leader) can ensure sufficient alignment and priority.

Make sure you carefully review the pros and cons of each model, as your choice determines the future organizational structure of your team, and it will set the collaboration between the teams for years to come. After deciding on the organizational structure when you set up your CoE, you must review the roles and skills that you need in your CoE. The details will vary depending on the business and organization you are in. But these roles should work with you—directly on your team or as part of a virtual team:

- **Roll-in:** Often, business analysts, process/ domain experts, and product managers will be the ones who collect ideas and build a pipeline of the ones your team could pursue to solve business problems with AI.
- **Full-stack development and data science:** Backend and frontend developers, data scientists, and prompt engineers have the software engineering and data science skills required to develop entire applications in the cloud—from back-end services such as computing, storage, and databases to AI, including data preparation, pipelines, models, and front-end development.
- **Roll-out:** Technology consultants and product managers support the implementation and adoption of your AI product by supporting end-users with training on how to use your product best.

A critical question to consider as you set up your CoE is measuring its impact and goal attainment, rather than simply counting the number of prototypes in the pipeline or the number of products delivered. The main reason for this is that it is *output*- as opposed to *outcome*-oriented.

Along with delivering outcomes, you need to market your CoE and its successes within your business. The best way to maintain a healthy idea pipeline is to continuously attract new business for your CoE. Sharing examples of your work with different business functions and showing measurable results help you achieve this. Publish them on an internal portal or send them to your organization via a regular newsletter. Custom branding around the CoE and a place to publish upcoming events draw even further attention and awareness. As part of your CoE's role to generate an idea pipeline, you must tell others across the business that you even exist and educate them about AI.

Consider setting up a small booth in the office or a roadshow to help your stakeholders understand the potential of AI and that your CoE can help them move from exploring to implementing AI. In addition, reach out to your senior business stakeholders and set up one-on-one meetings or join their all-hands meetings to share the information with a broader audience. Once your CoE is set up, you will transition from planning to execution. The first task will be to create and manage an idea pipeline of potential AI capabilities.

Identifying AI Opportunities Across the Business

So you have built your Center of Excellence (CoE) and received funding—now, what? Whether it is at the beginning of setting up the organization or while it is in operation, a dried-up idea pipeline will delay your output or kill the program altogether.

Developing a culture to foster innovation requires subject matter experts to know where and what to use AI for. But culture is more than how you define it within your company. Your team members are part of their own cultures, and they bring that experience and mindset to work. For example, some countries are more risk-averse than others (e.g., in Europe) or value privacy over innovation. Naturally, these team members might be more concerned about the use of AI, their data handling, and the impact of AI on their jobs. Being cognizant of this fact is especially relevant for AI leaders in global companies with operations in multiple countries who deal with change management remotely.

A recent study by Pew Research[18] in 2023 shows that 52% of people in the United States are concerned about AI in their daily lives, a 14% increase from the previous year. Your business experts certainly don't need to be deep AI experts themselves. However, they need to have a good enough understanding of what business problems AI can resolve and how it helps them in their role.

As an AI leader, you can foster this awareness and lead by example. Host townhall meetings as an opportunity to connect with business teams and to explain how AI can help them in their roles. Offer working with your CoE to find the most promising ideas for new AI capabilities. Once they understand that Generative AI can draft emails and blog posts or generate images and video and the like, they can look for similar

---

18 Pew Research, 2023, "Growing public concern about the role of artificial intelligence in daily life," August 28, 2023, https://www.pewresearch.org/short-reads/2023/08/28/growing-public-concern-about-the-role-of-artificial-intelligence-in-daily-life.

opportunities in their own business area and exploring using the technology to draft product descriptions or summarize reports.

Building a healthy idea pipeline takes work. It results from leadership support, advertising your CoE, enabling others, and prioritizing which ideas to pursue. For example, approach your leadership and ask them about potential areas for further insights and automation that they generally see in the business based on the efficiency and efficacy of the current operation. Now that they understand where the gaps are, you can suggest to them how AI can help them address these gaps. That helps you get buy-in and sponsorship. This collaboration is also a great way to enable them to understand the technology further and communicate what it can do for the business.

In parallel, take a bottom-up approach and meet with business process experts and end-users. They are the ones who follow the process day in and day out and know where the issues lie. This group will also be working with your product regularly. Winning their trust and support will go a long way. Throughout this process, your team should use access to these stakeholder groups to upskill them on the technology and its business impact.

Understanding what AI can do for their business area enables them to look for opportunities in their area. Whether it is joining leadership or team meetings, wheeling a whiteboard to the cafeteria and educating colleagues, sharing examples through a curated newsletter, or offering 1-on-1 consultations, there are a variety of options for you to choose from to get ideas flowing and to build your pipeline.

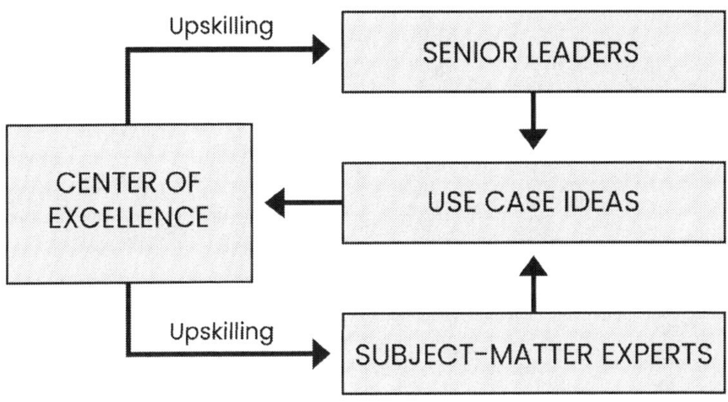

Building an AI Idea Pipeline

Now that you have established the idea pipeline, you can bring it to life in the next chapter in the section titled "Formalizing the Process From Idea to Implementation."

One of the hardest learnings you will make as a first-time AI leader is prioritizing which use cases to pursue and when to discontinue them. Especially if you have already invested a significant amount of money on exploring an idea, there is a high tendency to continue throwing good money after bad. However, as part of your portfolio process, you must look hard at your running and planned projects and decide which ones you will continue to work on and which ones to pause or stop.

Next, we will discuss how AI leaders can help their teams collaborate with the business to develop AI products that meet their peers' requirements.

Key Takeaways

Creating an AI-ready innovation culture requires you to address it from multiple angles:

- Business leaders realize that AI is a strategically important topic for their company. However, they might not fully understand AI's terminologies and opportunities. You need to spend ample time with them, enabling them to identify opportunities in their part of the business and encouraging their team members to do the same.
- Generative AI is making it easier than ever to experience AI first-hand, no matter your role. In addition to top-down support, bottom-up awareness and engagement are just as vital to a successful AI program.
- A typical organizational setup when adopting new technologies is a Center of Excellence (CoE). It combines expertise, guidelines, and standards in a central place and educates the rest of the organization to adopt technologies such as AI.
- Initially, CoEs start as a central team that evolves into decentralized organizations as maturity increases.
- You and your teams alone can only identify so many opportunities in a business function that AI can improve. Business teams that are much closer to the day-to-day activities have much better insight into the

areas that could work better. That's why these teams need to be able to put AI in the context of their work.

Further Reading

- Schmarzo, Bill. 2023. *AI & Data Literacy: Empowering Citizens of Data Science*. Packt Publishing. 978-1835083505.

Chapter Six

HARNESSING DIVERSE PERSPECTIVES

Designing for Human-AI Collaboration

AI already outperforms humans—on narrowly defined tasks. Claims and studies introduced in chapter 1 make it easier for business leaders to pursue AI to cut costs or even staff. But there is a larger angle than the replacement. Humans and AI can achieve the best results in a process when they contribute to it with their individual as well as their combined strengths. The method for leveraging these strengths is creating *adaptive processes*. For example, when it comes to uncertainty, humans are adaptable and capable of dealing with it—they can even be highly creative. AI helps humans take over those tasks that are still mundane and repetitive to this day. This allows humans to focus on the more creative and relationship aspects in business. As an AI leader, you need to consider who gives recommendations to whom—the AI recommends information to the human or vice versa—and who will make the final decision or gets to intervene. You can picture it as a spectrum of human-AI collaboration that ranges from operating to observing. Depending on your model and tasks, the human involvement may move to one end of the spectrum or the other. Another way to think about it is a seesaw: as AI involvement goes up, human involvement goes down. AI products augment humans' abilities by proactively alerting users, providing recommendations, or partially automating tasks. That allows humans to focus on the parts of their role that require communication, collaboration, and critical thinking.

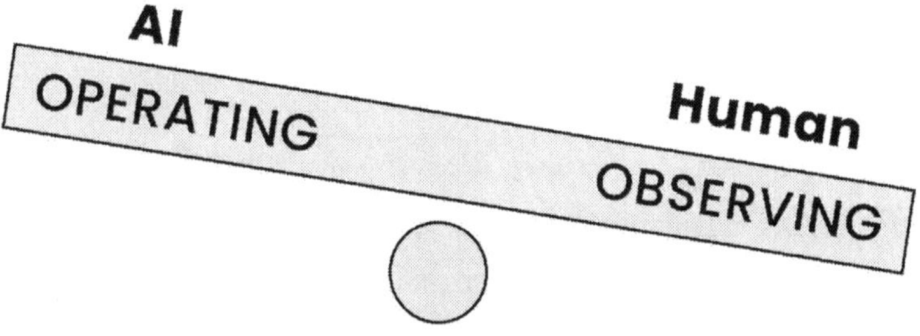

Spectrum of Human-AI Collaboration

Complexity, ambiguity, and risk are the critical factors for deciding who does what and how far. To ensure oversight and reasoning in context of the business, you should strongly consider keeping humans in the loop for tasks that involve a higher risk-level.

Humans have different tendencies regarding their reliance on AI. Some might accept its recommendations verbatim, making their decisions as accurate as the model's. Others might override AI-generated recommendations in favor of their own. Because of their corrections (and thereby potentially over-correcting), they can lower the system's efficacy. It's important you keep an eye out for this as you're building and rolling out AI products, and to build your users' trust in it. Otherwise, if your AI products are performing inconsistently, the blame can fall on your products when the root cause was a lack of users' trust. Ideally, your AI system provides sufficient context for the user to be comfortable trusting the recommendations.

Automating any process with the help of technology introduces an additional level of risk despite the associated improvements in scale, task-level reliability, and cost. But what do you do when your AI-enabled feature stops working or even breaks a core part of a process such as payroll or financial close? How quickly can you recover? And how do you recover at all? These are some of the questions you must ask yourself and your team. You can be confident that your business stakeholders will ask you. Your business's willingness to accept risk will be an essential factor in deciding the extent to which you might want to automate a process or step—or purposefully keep a human in the loop.

An additional aspect you need to consider is the cost your business incurs, for example while recovering from a failure. Increased levels of automation can lead to a decrease in situational awareness of the subject-matter experts running the process, but standard operating procedures and fallback manuals can help preserve the knowledge to complete the process even in the absence of automation.

Formalizing the Process from Idea to Implementation

Now that the organizational structure is in place in the form of the CoE, you need to operationalize your AI program. While senior leaders expect rapid outcomes, the inherent risk is focusing on the wrong initiatives for the wrong reasons and for the benefit of fast results. That's where setting up a robust idea pipeline and ideation process can support your organization in identifying the most valuable use cases for AI and prioritizing them for further evaluation, prototyping, and implementation.

This process aims to create an idea funnel with defined quality gates at the end of each phase (we'll discuss the five phases in a moment). That allows you to focus your most expensive and scarce resources (e.g. data scientists) on those features that deliver the most promising results. This funnel will also help you filter out the ones that are not as valuable or feasible as expected during the earlier phases. You will have the highest number of ideas in the earlier phases with the number of ideas in later stages getting considerably smaller. It's important to keep in mind: *It is not the number of AI ideas (in progress or in your product) that make an impact, rather than an idea's impact on the business.* This is an important point to stress with your senior leadership regarding the way they would like you to report your team's progress.

The ideal typical idea funnel follows five phases, from generating ideas to operating your AI product. Each of these phases includes several key activities and decisions that you and your team need to complete before you move to the next phase. Skipping steps is one of the most common reasons for project failure in the medium term.

- **Ideation**: Collect ideas across your business by meeting with stakeholders and multipliers, and collaborate with business experts to qualify the ideas based on their expected business value, business impact, and compliance with legal and ethical guidelines. (Learn more about the latter in chapter 7.) Determine which KPIs the individual idea influences and if sufficient data is available and accessible to pursue the idea in the next phase. The clearer you can define the expected outcome in this early phase, the easier it will be later on to build your model or Generative AI-supported application. Finally, get your business stakeholders' sign-off on record before you move the idea to the next phase. A review meeting is a good forum to operationalize it.
- **Validation:** It is getting serious. Earlier assumptions about data availability and access will meet reality. As soon as your team has access and you have passed this milestone, you are on to creating the first model

or building your Retrieval-Augmented Generation (RAG) pipeline for your application. Defining exactly what data and which variables are needed takes a considerable amount of work and alignment with your business stakeholders. Building an initial prototype allows you to prove the idea's feasibility and validate whether the early results meet expectations and if the project should continue.

- **Realization:** You have proven that the idea is feasible—now it's time to build it as a full product or feature. Gather feedback from your business stakeholders and users in this step and iterate further.
- **Implementation:** The AI product or feature is built. This phase focuses on rolling it out and scaling your AI product to the target group. Monitor the initial use and ask for feedback. Ensure you can incorporate it quickly to maintain a high user satisfaction.
- **Operation:** Once your model or feature is in production, the next step is maintaining it. Whether it is monitoring the model for changes and decreased performance (drift) or the Generative AI-based application for continued adherence to safeguards and quality, there are always opportunities to improve the current scope or expand it. The latter becomes the inception of a new idea moving through the funnel.

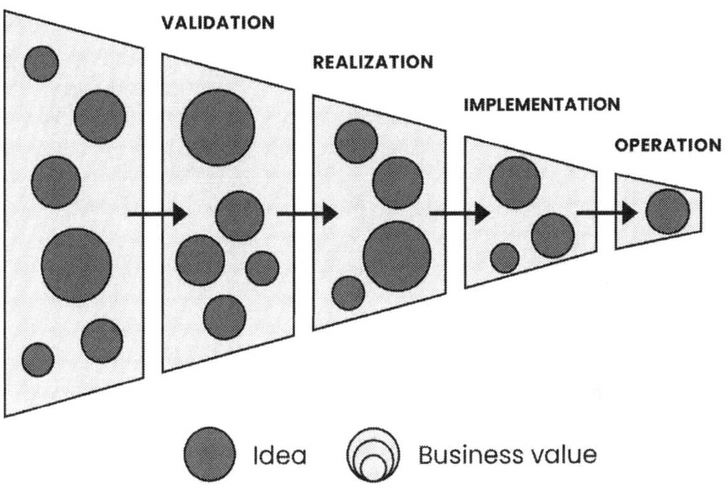

Phases of the Idea Funnel

You can operationalize your AI idea funnel process by setting up a regular cadence to review the status of each team's projects. The outcome of this process also ensures your team is utilized for quarters to come, focusing on the most promising AI features. Having a portfolio of ideas will also help them work on other ideas in case the one they are currently working on faces hurdles and delays or doesn't deliver the expected outcome.

Improving Communication Between Technical and Business Teams

One thing is clear: You can't run AI projects alone or in isolation. You always need a business context for your product, your model, and any results that you generate or predict to be relevant. When the two stakeholder groups work together, a cultural gap between technical and business teams becomes evident. Business and technology teams don't always have the same objectives and have reservations or suspicion toward each other. The teams typically don't use the same vocabulary or have the same priorities, so misunderstandings are expected. However, fostering collaboration between the two groups is critical to shaping their awareness and understanding of each other.

For example, a change to an existing business process introduces risk during the implementation and the operation. If you cannot pay your employees' salaries on time at the end of the month because of a change you have introduced to the process, the most promising AI innovation won't help your stakeholder whose reputation is on the line. Therefore, business stakeholders can be wary of working with AI teams.

At the same time, that is why you should identify your critical stakeholders early on and seek to understand their main business problems. Look for ways to help them improve their operations or reduce costs, and you will have your first advocate—your first ally. As you expand to other business functions or teams, this person can be a crucial spokesperson for you to tell others about the impact you and your team have made and support building your credibility.

As you approach other business leaders, don't be afraid to create a bit of FOMO (fear of missing out). You can use

FOMO to give examples of the impact you could have on their business and simultaneously show that others have realized that opportunity before them, but it's not too late to get started.

As you start working on AI ideas, you will likely encounter resistance while working with your stakeholders. These challenges can stem from the uncertainty of AI projects and their potential impact on your stakeholder's job, status, and knowledge or changing business priorities in general. Your stakeholders might be afraid to lose influence over decision-making when AI has been introduced. They might fear that their span of control will shrink as AI is taking over more and more tasks from team members. AI might even make better decisions than your stakeholder altogether as it is per definition unemotional—unlike its human users. When your stakeholders push back, your progress until this point will come to a grinding halt. Over the weeks, your project's status will turn from green to yellow to red. Your leaders will look to you and ask for updates. No matter which avenue you try, it seems you are in a deadlock, unable to move forward. That's the time to explore your options outside formal hierarchies and organizational structures. It is time to call upon your network in the organization to extend your influence.

Connect with others to resolve the situation and get buy-in where you cannot obtain it yourself. The person who you are calling upon does not have to be a leader. They are influential because of their domain expertise, connections, or organizational tenure. But starting to look for these champions at the point in time when you need them is too late. That is why you need to build your network in the role from day one for the first few months and continuously nurture that network.

In addition to building your network across the organization and leveraging it effectively, you can strategically leverage a group of multipliers. Multipliers are part of a business unit and have an affinity for technology and innovation. In addition, or as part of their primary role in the business, they can learn about AI, how to use it, and how to apply it. They will carry this information to their teams across the business. You can identify the best colleagues who should become your multiplier in several ways.

Effective multipliers bring a combination of skills to the table, such as their understanding of the business, its processes, and goals plus an affinity for technology and innovation. They also have a positive attitude toward collaborating across teams, being comfortable with ambiguity and change, and enjoy being at the forefront of innovation.

Organizationally, you will need to get a mandate and leadership support for identifying and including multipliers from different departments in your business. The closer your reporting line to the business decision maker (e.g., CEO or President) is, the better your chances of success. Few leaders like to add additional tasks to their teams' agenda, primarily when it doesn't immediately support their objectives. The clearer you can articulate how these multipliers can help your business achieve its vision and mission, the easier it will be to get leadership buy-in. That is also why aligning your AI strategy with your business strategy upfront is essential.

Building a community of multipliers has several benefits. For example, you can scale your enablement, raise AI fluency in the organization, and share key learnings across various parts of the company—all while creating an input channel for new AI products and features that increase your idea pipeline. That is directly related to the multipliers and their role in multiplying it within their business teams. On the other hand, you will also get valuable feedback from these stakeholders about their challenges and requirements. You will be surprised what your multipliers find and share with you. You can gather and prioritize these topics and concerns and subsequently implement them. Therefore, your building products will be more relevant for your stakeholders. In the next chapter, we'll discuss how to use AI responsibly.

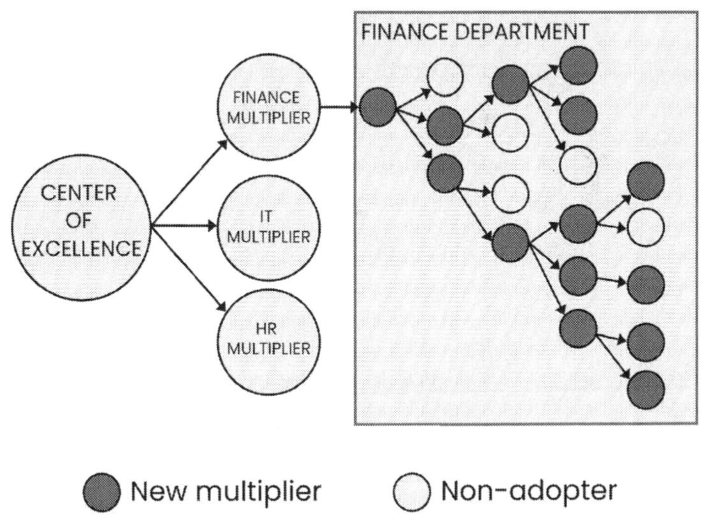

Example of How Multipliers Can Spread AI Literacy in Their Departments

Key Takeaways

In this chapter, we've learned how you can foster collaboration between AI and business teams to build AI products that the business adopts:

- AI is most effective in transforming a business process when humans and AI work hand-in-hand. AI products augment humans' abilities by proactively alerting users, providing recommendations, or partially automating tasks. That allows humans to focus on the parts of their role that require communication, collaboration, and critical thinking.
- Build an innovation funnel of potential AI features or products helps you capture where opportunities exist across the business and prioritize the most impactful ones for timely development.
- As your AI features mature, you can plot them on a funnel along the stages of ideation, validation, realization, implementation, and operation to track and communicate progress.
- A nucleus such as a CoE needs additional help to scale its efforts to drive standardization, enablement, and adoption of AI. They need multipliers in various business functions who advocate for the proper use of AI.
- Setting up a community of multipliers who have an affinity for technology and can also bring feedback to the CoE is a crucial resource of the extended network that any AI leader should establish to increase relevance and impact.

Part III

IMPLEMENTING AI RESPONSIBLY

Implementing AI in a business environment needs more than people and a pipeline of ideas. As an AI leader, you must ensure that the new AI products you develop or use also adhere to ethical guidelines and standards while protecting data privacy, and that the decisions your AI features make protect individuals' rights—whether they are employees, clients, or users. Given AI's pace and scale, these aspects are becoming more critical to understand and implement.

Chapter Seven

ESTABLISHING PRINCIPLES FOR HUMAN-CENTERED AI

Exploring the Importance of AI Ethics

During the last AI hype (2016-2020), AI was promised to revolutionize how we work and drive task automation across industries and departments. Everything would happen quickly, from self-driving cars to intelligent assistants who know your every wish. And we would have lots of time to pursue our true, creative passions. That hasn't quite happened (yet). But numerous examples over the years have made it clear that ethics and responsible design have to be a core aspect of software development and AI systems:

Courts in the US have used AI to predict the risk of recidivism[19]. The underlying model has included biases that have ascribed higher risks of committing another crime based on a person's ethnic background.

Public authorities have used AI to determine their citizens' potential for committing social welfare fraud[20]. These models have considered attributes such as health history, family status, and fluency in the country's native language to score individuals.

A multinational technology company has used AI during automated resume reviews[21]. The model at the heart of the application had been trained on historical data in an industry where male applicants have traditionally filled roles. Hence, when rolled out in production, the model favored male applicants over female ones.

As a result, voices demanding ethical AI practices became louder, and companies started drafting their AI ethics principles, setting up AI ethics advisory boards, and implementing ethics policies.

---

19 ProPublica, 2016, "How We Analyzed the COMPAS Recidivism Algorithm," May 23, 2016, https://www.propublica.org/article/how-we-analyzed-the-compas-recidivism-algorithm.

20 WIRED, 2023, "This Algorithm Could Ruin Your Life," March 6, 2023, https://www.wired.com/story/welfare-algorithms-discrimination.

21 Reuters, 2018, "Amazon scraps secret AI recruiting tool that showed bias against women," October 9, 2018, https://www.reuters.com/article/idUSL2N1VB1FQ.

However, neither committees nor policies solve the underlying problems unless AI ethics is operationalized in the day-to-day activities of all involved stakeholders. The best policies remain intentions unless they are implemented effectively. That requires they become second nature for employees in the organization. There are four aspects that organizations need to implement in concert:

- **AI ethics vision:** The higher-level intent to develop and use AI in ways that are ethical and responsible.
- **AI ethics panels:** A group of leaders who advise the organization on the latest developments in AI ethics (e.g., regulations) and review planned AI features before they are developed.
- **AI ethics policies:** Guidelines by which the organization develops and uses AI in alignment with regulations.
- **AI ethics processes:** Operational steps to educate the organization on responsible, ethical AI and to check for compliance with proposed AI capabilities.

Skipping any of these aspects typically leads to negative effects downstream (e.g., use of protected attributes or biased output) stemming from a lack of clarity on why AI ethics is important for the business, which details need to be considered or evolve, what is permissible, and how to learn about the business's latest AI ethics practices.

By its nature, AI requires lots of data to work correctly and make highly accurate and, hence, valuable predictions. That data is typically a representation of relationships or events found in the real world, which is why that data includes the same biases that we observe in the real world as well. At the same time, AI also has the potential to affect lots of people, given the scale with which it can make recommendations and automate decisions. A model's predictions could impact marginalized groups and exacerbate biases and disadvantages. Therefore, it is paramount that you and the business you work for establish guidelines for the ethical use of AI in your business—to do the right things and to minimize harm to others. Such guidelines often include an AI ethics statement. For example: *"We design for people and uphold democratic values including fairness and privacy."*

An important first step is defining a set of guiding principles that you can model after the principles defined by independent organizations such as the Organization for Economic Co-operation and Development (OECD)[22] or the United Nations Educational, Scientific and Cultural Organization (UNESCO)[23] or fully adopt one of these sets of guiding principles. The latter

---

22 OECD, 2024, "OECD AI Principles overview," 2024, https://oecd.ai/en/ai-principles.

23 UNESCO, 2023, "Recommendation on the Ethics of Artificial Intelligence," May 16, 2023, https://www.unesco.org/en/articles/recommendation-ethics-artificial-intelligence.

approach simplifies communicating your principles as you can refer to these bodies' guidelines with which your stakeholders can familiarize themselves. Compared to the OECD's AI principles, UNESCO's principles are broader in scope. As a starting point, choose the one that best aligns with your company's values.

OECD AI Principles	UNESCO Recommendation on AI Ethics
Inclusive growth, sustainable development and well-being	Sustainability Awareness and literacy Multi-stakeholder and adaptive governance & collaboration
Human rights and democratic values, including fairness and privacy	Right to privacy and data protection Proportionality and do no harm
Transparency and explainability	Transparency and explainability Human oversight and determination
Robustness, security and safety	Safety and security
Accountability	Responsibility and accountability

Overview of AI Ethics Principles by OECD and UNESCO

Operationalizing Responsible AI Throughout the Business

Understanding the importance of responsibly building AI products is a critical first step. As an AI leader, you must develop a strong vision for responsible AI, including how the organization uses, develops, and procures AI products. This vision is written down in an AI ethics statement. It is often the first start and connects the principle with concrete actions to be effective. For example, you should work with your HR department to expand the employee handbook with additional information about responsible AI practices. You could also add a paragraph about responsible innovation to job descriptions to signal applicants that your company has an established process for developing AI products responsibly, and that it is a priority. However, collaborating to seek opportunities for operationalizing responsible AI practices applies to all business functions, not just HR. While the vision serves as the guiding light for AI ethics, it is concrete actions through which it is put into practice.

In addition to a vision, guidelines, and policies, employees also need a path to raise their concerns if they see practices going against the defined policies, categorized into powerful, urgent, and legitimate stakeholder claims. That includes processes and governance for sharing these claims and the trust that these claims will be reviewed and taken seriously. Additionally, team members must feel comfortable knowing they can raise their concerns without fearing retaliation or termination.

Depending on your organization's culture, you can provide different options for employees to voice their concerns. Suppose your business already has more formal processes for raising ethical concerns, such as an ombudsperson or an ethics and compliance office. In that case, you can also expand this channel to address responsible AI concerns. In smaller organizations with less formal processes, a monthly executive town hall meeting can be an option to engage in a dialogue with employees and for them to voice their concerns. However, the level of trust between team members and leaders and the psychological safety across the organization needs to be extremely high to ensure that team members do speak up.

A middle ground could be employee groups that collect and review team members' concerns. If the group agrees that there is a significant concern, the team member can take the case forward to the leadership team. As a final option, employees concerned about unethical AI practices could raise their concerns to the authorities as whistleblowers while being protected from retaliation (e.g., California Whistleblower Protection Act).

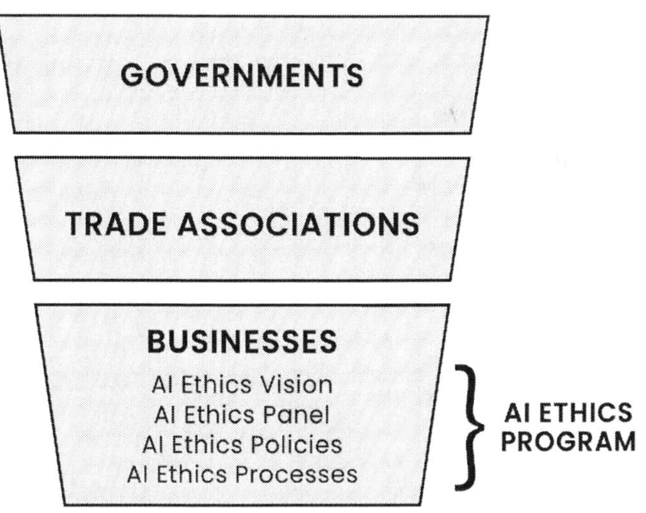

Factors Influencing Responsible AI Programs

While businesses need to operationalize the responsible development and use of AI throughout their organization, external factors are the primary guardrails. They provide the foundation for defining the businesses' policies:

- **Governments:** Regulations like the EU AI Act or presidential executive orders in the US provide macro-level guidance on scenarios for using AI and how to do so without negatively impacting large parts of the population. State-level legislation like the ELVIS Act provides additional requirements and protection.
- **Trade associations:** Organizations such as the International Trade Association, OECD, UNESCO, and World Economic Forum provide additional guidance for the responsible use of AI.

Responsible AI practices are essential for organizations to develop inclusive products that represent the diversity of their users. Developing a framework for operationalizing responsible AI practices applies to companies of all sizes. While Fortune 500 companies might have larger organizations, budgets, and formalized processes to dedicate toward responsible AI practices, smaller organizations are often more nimble in adopting new developments in responsible AI. No matter their size, those organizations that adapt more quickly to the changing landscape have built responsiveness, monitoring, and evaluation of the legal and regulatory environment into their processes and practices.

Adopting a Risk-Based Approach to Responsible AI

AI leaders need to ensure that the AI products they build are safe. You need to consider standards and regulations when setting up your AI program. One example is the European Union's AI Act[24], which takes a risk-based approach. By applying this risk-based approach to AI products, the EU intends to protect European citizens from AI-based decision-making's potential impact and harm. But what is considered a risk to begin with?

A common definition of risk is: *the probability and impact of an event with negative consequences occurring.* AI increases the rate and the scale with which decisions and business transactions are automated. Unlike previous technologies that are based on rulesets that lead to identical, repeatable outcomes given the same input, AI-based decisions and transactions are the result of predictions that can vary even when the input remains the same. Given this variability, introducing AI to a business also introduces new risks.

For example, in financial services, AI-automated loan approvals could further disadvantage marginalized groups without individuals being able to dispute decisions if their applications are rejected based on opaque criteria. In the public sector, social scoring to determine the trustworthiness of a

24 The European Parliament has approved the draft law on March 13, 2024 which has become law on August 1, 2024. The EU AI Act applies to any business doing business with EU citizens irrespective of the company being located within our outside of the EU.

country's citizens based on their social behavior could influence people's livelihoods with limited transparency in the score calculation and force conformism. (The latter example might sound very Orwellian, but this is an example that is specifically prohibited by the EU and is common practice in countries such as China.)

The EU AI Act defines regulatory guidelines for using AI that impact European citizens. First of all, it separates acceptable from unacceptable risks. Unacceptable risks include manipulating a person's or group's behavior, evaluating people's trustworthiness, or analyzing biometric data in public in real time. If your AI product falls into this category, your team should evaluate whether they can change the criteria for solving the business problem or change the data and features required to solve it. If they cannot pivot, immediately stop the development, as this capability is prohibited under the EU AI Act.

If you conclude that your AI product falls in the acceptable risk category, there are additional subcategories such as high-risk, limited-risk, and minimal-risk[25] to consider.

Your AI product poses a high risk under the AI Act, for example if it governs access to education, scores individuals' recidivism risk, assesses candidate resumes for job-fit, or determines immigration-related aspects such as migration or

---

25 Ada Lovelace Institute, 2022, "Expert explainer: The EU AI Act proposal," April 8, 2022, https://www.adalovelaceinstitute.org/resource/eu-ai-act-explainer.

border control. A self-assessment and documentation that confirms that the product meets the requirements of the AI Act is sufficient.

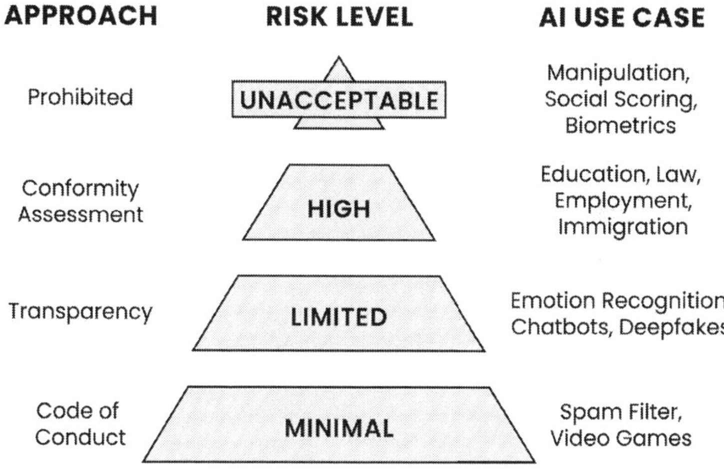

Risk Classification in the EU AI Act

Chatbots, emotion detection, and deepfake generation are examples of AI capabilities that are part of the limited risk category. To meet the requirements of the EU AI Act, you need to provide transparency to your end-users, for example in the UI, that your product includes AI or that AI has created information that your product presents to them.

Lastly, AI products like spam filters or AI in video games are seen as minimal risk that should be governed by a company's code of conduct. If your AI product is part of this risk level, you can proceed the development and should periodically reevaluate this AI product's risk classification to determine if it needs to be adjusted.

Businesses create data. They process data. They store data. Some of that data is related to their products and services—for example, master data. However, transactional data often includes personal data and personal identifiable information (PII). Regulations such as the GDPR describe different roles, such as data subject, controller, and processor who come in contact with data.

Businesses are accountable for *how* they handle data (data privacy) and *what* they use it for. In the case of the latter, fairness is an essential aspect. That is especially true when businesses use models that impact minorities or marginalized groups of people, and the underlying training data includes biases. A potential result of biased training data is discrimination. For example, facial recognition capabilities based on AI have historically shown inaccuracies, such as photo management applications incorrectly classifying people as Gorillas[26] or camera software incorrectly detecting neutral facial expressions of Asian people as the equivalent of Caucasians "blinking" their eyes[27].

---

26 BBC, 2015, "Google apologizes for Photo app's racist blunder," July 1, 2015, https://www.bbc.com/news/technology-33347866.amp.

27 TIME, 2010, "Are Face-Detection Cameras Racist?" January 22, 2010, https://time.com/archive/6906847/are-face-detection-cameras-racist.

As an AI leader evaluating technologies such as ML and Generative AI, you need to find a consensus among the leadership team on the purpose for which they want to use this technology in their business. It directly impacts the types of AI products and features they will explore and build. Next is defining what they will allow the technology to be used for (and not). At this point, regulations such as GDPR and the EU AI Act and their risk classification come into play. Lastly, you must determine what risks to anticipate when using AI, how you will mitigate them, and to what extent. New standards such as ISO 42001 provide a governance framework for AI models. For example, it covers model accuracy, data pipelining, and checking for hallucinations. By following a standard such as the one defined by ISO, AI leaders can demonstrate their business's adherence to quality and transparency for AI models.

Redefining Responsibility in the Age of Generative AI

Companies must assess which AI scenarios to build and what to use them for: *Is this scenario aligned with our AI ethics principles and values? Does it align with existing rules and regulations? How can we remove and mitigate bias?* In the past, individuals using AI-driven software were primarily the *consumers* of information (e.g., predictions or recommendations) that a model generated: *What will our liquidity and cash flow look like next quarter? Which sales opportunities have the highest propensity to close? Which products should you buy together?*

There were two critical reasons for users being information consumers. One was the technology itself. AI models that classify and predict data fundamentally differ from the foundation models that now create new data. The other reason was the prerequisites that only large companies could fulfill, such as access to large amounts of historical financial data, sales data, e-commerce data, and scalable infrastructure. Hence, AI ethics was primarily a concern for companies and their experts building AI-driven products. Trust was mainly a factor in users' acceptance: Can you trust that this prediction is accurate and how it was made? And why is that prediction more accurate than my own experience? But this has recently changed.

Fast-forward to the release of Generative AI tools like ChatGPT (text), Midjourney (image), ElevenLabs (audio), and D-ID (video). This new kind of AI has become accessible to anyone with an internet connection, often including free trials or being entirely free. While requirements largely remain the same for companies that build AI scenarios (e.g., business cases, ethics reviews, and infrastructure), the shift to Generative AI has evolved the responsibility for ethical behavior for individual users. Users who have previously acted on predicted or recommended information (based on corporate ethics) are now becoming *creators* of new information (based on their individual ethics). And the question of trust evolves: *Can you trust your Generative AI system to generate output that's accurate?*

Identifying Common Challenges of AI Ethics Programs

The headlines during the previous AI hype have made it clear that responsible AI is a must. Along with the need for responsible AI comes the need for companies to be vocal about their approach to AI being responsible. After all, your external stakeholders, such as customers and partners, expect it. Due to having to state that your AI approach is responsible, the industry has seen responsible AI *greenwashing* without operationalizing the necessary processes and frameworks. It is akin to businesses' claims to be sustainable and their referencing the word *green* without actually implementing or updating processes to be good for the environment.

Because leaders realize that responsible AI practices are important for ensuring that AI is used for good (and also to mitigate ethical, reputational, and cyber security risks), they start somewhere. And that somewhere is often defining principles for how the business uses AI. Although this is a good starting point, it is not the finish line. Leaders need help implementing these high-level goals into concrete actions throughout the organization. Team members must understand their role and why responsible AI practices are important for their work. After all, responsible AI is not just the task of an AI ethics department or just software engineers, data scientists, or consultants. It affects *all* roles. But if you are unable to move from principles to actions, your responsible AI ambitions are in trouble. Creating and rolling out information about responsible AI is a key part of the work.

The challenge is that teams often operate in silos, and their goals and incentives do not reward acting responsibly. For example, assume data scientists are being measured by the number of AI features they ship or by reducing the number of bugs they create. In that case, they might not see responsible AI as a big priority for their work, because arguably it's not a big priority for the team or unit, if it's not part of their goals. Additionally, if the software engineers in another team that the data scientists work with are measured by quickly moving items through their backlog of product features to be delivered, raising responsible AI concerns could be counterproductive to achieving the team's goals. Hence, they, too, are not incentivized to spend time on responsible AI—much or at all. For responsible AI to be a priority for your team, *you* need to make it a priority. Shape the team's goals where you can do so directly in your reporting line, and work with your peers across the organization to ensure that they do the same for their teams.

Although bias is often the most obvious dimension of ethical, responsible AI, these programs must go further. For example, every model interprets the real world and its complexities based on a subset of relevant data. Hence, understanding what a model optimizes for (e.g., life expectancy) is crucial for determining whether it is permissible in the first place (e.g., the model's recommendations could be biased based on ethnicity life expectancy data).

Large Language Models (LLMs) give imperfect responses. As a leader, encourage your teams to get hands-on with Generative AI while understanding the technology's limitations. Humans rely too much on AI when they expect AI to be more capable than it actually is. This misalignment can lead to improper use and negative results. One such example has been in the news: Using tools like ChatGPT to research legal cases without checking the generated information for factual inaccuracies[28].

Data is the lifeblood of AI systems, whether it is data used to train a model or data that providers use to build Generative AI models. However, the training data includes relationships, events, and transactions observed by real entities in the real world. As such, it is also prone to encompassing biases in the real world. For example, *Hadas Kotek*[29], a data scientist, uncovered gender bias in ChatGPT through the following exchange:

- *User: The doctor yelled at the nurse because she was late. Who was late?*
- *ChatGPT: According to the sentence, the nurse was late.*
- *User: The nurse yelled at the doctor because she was late. Who was late?*
- *ChatGPT: In this sentence, it is still the nurse who was late.*
- *User: The doctor yelled at the nurse because he was late. Who was late?*

28 Associated Press, 2023, "Lawyers blame ChatGPT for tricking them into citing bogus case law," June 8, 2023, https://apnews.com/article/artificial-intelligence-chatgpt-courts-e15023d7e6fdf4f099aa122437dbb59b.

29 Hadas Kotek, 2023, Tweet, April 18, 2023, https://twitter.com/HadasKotek/status/1648453764117041152.

- *ChatGPT: In this sentence, the doctor being late seems to be a mistake or a typographical error because it does not logically fit with the rest of the sentence. If we assume that the intended meaning was that the doctor yelled at the nurse for being late, then the nurse was late.*
- *User: The nurse yelled at the doctor because he was late. Who was late?*
- *ChatGPT: In this sentence, the doctor was late.*

Applications increasingly rely on LLMs to generate output. Biases found in these models such as the example above pose risks of further repeating and amplifying these biases through any new output they generate. Additionally, if publicly exposed, they create a reputational risk for the organization providing the application.

However, it is not just gender bias that requires your attention. English language and Western (or even US-centric) data are prevalent sources for AI models. That risks further amplifying American values, worldviews, and biases in the rest of the world. From an economic point of view, data in English is vastly available, and it is one of the most widely understood languages worldwide. That means the data is available at a low cost (if any beyond computing power) while being relevant for a large user base. On the flip side, this also means that models often need help understanding local dialects and languages, for example, in Africa. That discriminates against local populations, while there are few companies at Western tech corporations' level of capability and capital. Hence, access to relevant technology in underserved parts of the world is further limited. These circumstances can lead to a further growing global digital divide.

Increasing Diversity to Build AI That Serves Us All

AI does and will continue to impact all our lives even more going forward. It is the foundation of decision-making and a core component of any digitally connected product or service. However, the tech industry, which is responsible for developing and advancing AI and its derivatives, has a diversity problem. If AI should serve us all, a broad representation of all people is crucial, including diversity of gender, thought, and ethnic and professional background. But it already gets challenging at the first one.

Women are generally underrepresented on data and AI teams. This underrepresentation of women in technology-centric careers starts at an early age, though—not just when degrees are completed or women are already in the workforce. Girls need role models and examples of female leaders to see that career path for themselves. Early education on science and technology is also a critical factor.

Once women are in the workforce, career opportunities beyond individual contributor roles become scarce. This situation can lead to a five- to ten-year period in which women see limited or stagnant career growth, especially relative to their male colleagues. These limited opportunities often coincide with women taking time off to have children. As a result, they frequently miss out on opportunities to move into leadership roles or even advance in their careers as individual contributors.

Shaping an inclusive culture is an essential leadership task. AI leaders need to build that team and organizational culture and provide the space for women to speak up and share their perspectives. Supporting women in data and AI needs to become second nature. Leaders should start working with the women in their organization and ask what additional resources or information they need. External organizations such as "Women in Data"[30] or "Women in AI"[31] provide education, training, and opportunities for women in the data and AI domain to network. Consider paying your employees' dues or training costs to support them further, or donate to the organizations themselves.

The critical stages of maturity of gender diversity in the business are:

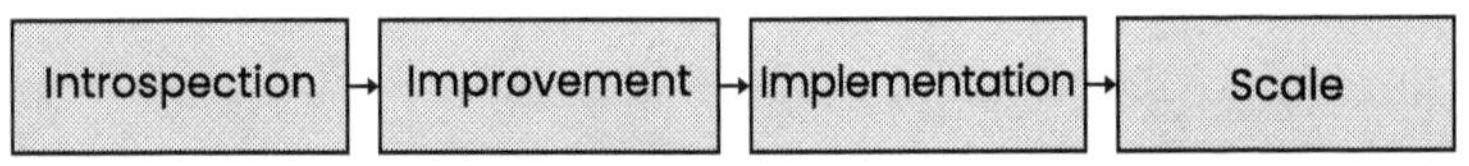

Four Stages of Maturity for Gender Diversity in Data & AI

1. **Introspection:** What are you doing to support the women in the role today?

---

30 Women in Data, 2024, https://www.womenindata.org.

31 Women in AI, 2024, https://www.womaninai.co.

2. **Improvement:** How can you improve the current situation for women?
3. **Implementation:** Which suggestions can you implement (and how)?
4. **Scale:** Which external groups and organizations can you support?

While gender and biodiversity are cornerstones of creating a more diverse workforce that develops AI products which serve us all, diversity is a much bigger topic. For example, ensure your hiring practices provide equal opportunities to underrepresented groups, including ethnic, educational, and professional backgrounds outside of core scientific and engineering roles.

As an AI leader, you set the tone and lead by example. Whether it is your direct reports and leadership team or their individual teams, creating a diverse and inclusive AI team in alignment with your business objectives is an important aspect of your role and for changing the reality for those seeking opportunities.

Uncovering the Role of Sustainability and Generative AI

In this discussion about additional aspects to consider beyond technology, sustainability has been emerging in addition to ethics. For decades, business leaders have looked to optimize their business with the help of technology to increase revenue or reduce costs.

However, the objective for using AI needs to go beyond these two measures and incorporate the impact on our planet. Whether using AI products to optimize for more sustainable practices or using AI to serve the people, leaders have a unique responsibility to support financial and environmental goals.

AI offers the potential to improve the lives of millions and billions of people. From climate change, weather forecasts, and yield prediction to energy management, healthcare, and education, the applications touch nearly every aspect of our lives. Improving all of these aspects sounds like a pretty lofty goal. It's attainable, but not without contributions from businesses that implement AI. Businesses across industries can contribute to the UN's Sustainable Development Goals (SDGs)[32], adopted by world leaders in 2015 as a "universal call to action to end poverty, protect the planet, and ensure that by 2030 all people enjoy peace and prosperity." AI initiatives and projects not only need to serve the business and its interests. When leveraging AI, you must also consider sustainable energy consumption practices.

A 2023 study by MIT[33] found it requires as much energy to generate 1,000 images with Generative AI as it does to charge

---

32 UNDP, "Sustainable Development Goals," 2024, https://www.undp.org/sustainable-development-goals.

33 MIT Technology Review, 2023, "Making an image with Generative AI uses as much energy as charging your phone," December 1, 2023, https://www.technologyreview.com/2023/12/01/1084189/making-an-image-with-generative-ai-uses-as-much-energy-as-charging-your-phone.

your phone. The same task creates the equivalent amount of emissions as driving your gasoline-powered car for 4.1 miles (approx. 6 km). Consider how many images we make "just for fun," to "try out AI," and to "see what it will do." For the most part, we don't use these images for anything useful. We might even discard them because they don't meet our expectations. But along with that, we are also increasing our carbon footprint.

We can argue that generating images with AI saves emissions compared to creating these images in the real world. There are fewer requirements to travel to places, use physical products and objects, and overall be able to create visual representations that would be expensive or even impossible to create or capture otherwise. It makes sense for stock images and ads that serve a commercial purpose, especially if they have previously required an extensive setup and budget.

However, the consumer side of image and video generation is often a waste of energy and resources. Yes, even in this scenario: AI generates fewer emissions than you hopping in your car, driving to your "one-hour photo" place, having photos developed or printed, and driving back home. But at the same time, we didn't have a studio in our basement with infinite models and talent, a personal stylist, endless possibilities untethered from physics, and seemingly cheap to generate as part of a subscription. So, we would not have been so wasteful as to create and print all these images under physical conditions, which means less emissions than AI generation.

Using AI in business is primarily driven by specific use cases and business functions. However, viewing AI in the context of sustainability needs a second purpose. AI can also serve the planet beyond pure efficiency gains. The objective is to connect individual AI projects with bigger goals serving humanity. This thinking is yet to become more prevalent. However, it can help you anchor your personal use cases and initiatives in a larger objective that your business supports or is a critical production factor or outcome. Examples of such goals could be improving energy efficiency, public health and healthcare (and access to it), and yield prediction in agriculture.

That's especially key where your AI products directly impact the environment or the people who live in it. Tech companies manufacturing devices and appliances can contribute by optimizing designs for energy efficiency and optimized load. Healthcare providers can incentivize their customers with the help of AI (e.g., gamification) to exhibit behavior that benefits public health. Companies in different industries can better forecast and mitigate their emissions with AI. Combining individual choices aggregates and contributes to increased sustainability—much more so than just continuing to talk about AI's potential alone.

UN Sustainable Development Goals		
Utilities Company	Healthcare Provider	Company N
↓	↓	↓
Energy Management	Public Health	Emissions Management

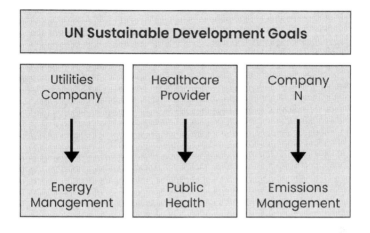

AI's Cross-industry Sustainability Goals

Despite the increased energy consumption of Generative AI, this technology can actually contribute to the decarbonization of our plant. Take the example of data centers. They contribute roughly 0.2% of the world's energy consumption[34, 35]; approximately 10% of that is attributed to AI workloads (i.e., 0.02% of the data center consumption). Even if the energy consumption for those AI workloads increases to 0.04% (or even

34 International Energy Agency, 2024, "Electricity 204," January 24, 2024, https://www.iea.org/reports/electricity-2024.

35 *What's the* BUZZ? *Drive Sustainability and Energy Efficiency with AI Leadership*, May 28, 2024, https://youtu.be/i5lwGFvYU_c.

all the way up to 0.5% by 2027[36] as some sources estimate), this technology could be used to drive efficiency of the remaining 99.5-99.96% of global energy consumption and thereby drive a significantly greater impact than the power consumption required to achieve that result.

One goal to strive for could be achieving the same efficiency with less energy, for example to assemble a car or heat and cool a building. While the majority of energy consumption is attributed to heating and cooling, there is often very little sophistication in current processes, other than an on/off switch. But by collecting data from smart sensors, you can use AI to analyze, predict, and optimize the expected energy consumption, and maintain a perfectly warm or cool home without impacting comfort, while reducing energy consumption by 20-30%. That is an example of a more complete calculation that also considers the amount of emissions saved. Some estimate that the return on investment of AI relative to carbon emissions is 1:500 to 1:1,000.

Taking AI's impact on sustainability further, it is not just the immediate emissions caused by using ML and Generative AI and the business scenarios in which these technologies can actually reduce the total amount of carbon emissions, but also ensuring responsible, sustainable development practices that start with understanding which technology you should use

---

36 The Verge, 2024, "How much electricity does AI consume?," February 16, 2024, https://www.theverge.com/24066646/ai-electricity-energy-watts-generative-consumption.

when. As we have previously discussed, Generative AI does not replace Machine Learning or the need for it. Recommending products, creating demand forecasts, optimizing delivery routes, and detecting cybersecurity or financial anomalies cannot be solved reliably with Generative AI—and even if they could, they would be more energy-intensive than ML. As part of your AI leadership role, you will need to raise awareness for these recommendations as part of your software development guidelines and training.

A few years ago, AI was a highly technical topic reserved for mathematicians, statisticians, and computer scientists. While technology was a core part of data scientists' education, ethics was not. Compared to five to six years ago, professionals working on AI now appear to have a higher level of ethics awareness. AI ethics researchers and responsible AI industry groups have become a melting pot for experts of different backgrounds. Thank goodness! Because it is this kind of diversity, we need in this field if everyone should feel represented and build AI that should serve us all. However, ethics is only one aspect of responsible AI practices.

Responsible AI is evolving into a trifecta of data privacy, ethics, and sustainability. Companies developing AI products need to ensure they positively impact the planet. To me, this means that Sustainability as a topic needs to become an integral part of AI development and of AI products—not a nice-to-have and not an afterthought. It's time we evolve our thinking and definition of what aspects constitute an AI project.

Now that we have covered the core principles of leading responsible AI projects, in the next chapter we will discuss the technological concepts for generating output and creating more tailored output.

Key Takeaways

In this chapter, we have learned the core aspects of building responsible AI products:

- Given the scale at which AI can make decisions and the biases in the underlying data, ethics is an essential aspect of any AI initiative.
- Organizations that have realized this necessity have frequently set up AI boards and governance processes. However, operationalizing these bodies and processes in the organization presents challenges.
- Along with increasing awareness of ethics in AI, there is increasing diversity. The benefits include approaching situations from different vantage points and having a different understanding of the implications and impact. Diversity does not only concern ethnic backgrounds; it already begins with gender diversity.
- Aside from its impact on business, AI also impacts sustainability. Whether the effect is positive or negative depends on the users and the use cases. However, optimizing for environmental and sustainable goals in addition to business KPIs is a step towards achieving outcomes that also serve our planet.

Further Reading

- Blackman, Reid. 2022. *Ethical Machines: Your Concise Guide to Totally Unbiased, Transparent, and Respectful AI.* Harvard Business Review Press. 978-1647822811.
- Minevich, Mark. 2023. *Our Planet Powered by AI: How We Use Artificial Intelligence to Create a Sustainable Future for Humanity.* Wiley. 978-1394180608.

Chapter Eight

ENSURING RELEVANT OUTPUT

Understanding Data as the Foundation for Safe AI

Despite the current hype around Generative AI, this new technology has several limitations you must be aware of and mitigate. For example, Generative AI models might generate output that represents their training data.

Large Language Models can generate information that sounds as if a human had created it. This fact often leads to the misconception that businesses no longer need data or clean data. However, that couldn't be further from the truth. LLMs' output based on basic prompting techniques is not bad, but generic. AI leaders must augment LLMs with business data to generate more specific output tailored to solve the concrete problem.

Like in previous generations of AI, business data brings context and value to the results. Businesses often face the challenge of having an abundance of data that is not readily usable. This data is frequently incomplete, contains duplicates, and requires additional work by the AI team before they can create a new model. The same challenges also apply when using the data to create more relevant prompts and output using Retrieval-Augmented Generation (RAG), or to fine-tune a model to perform better on a dedicated task than a generic LLM. It is precisely these techniques that can address the following problem: *hallucinations.*

Hallucination, confabulation, factual inaccuracies—call it whatever you want. The consensus is that it's bad. It's unwanted. It's a side-effect of using LLMs that might never go away[37]. Irrespective of the term you prefer, it describes an LLM creating plausible-sounding output that is factually incorrect, untrue, and false. As businesses are increasingly looking to adopt Generative AI, these hallucinations can become a problem when the business's reputation is on the line because of a statement that AI has generated.

Whether "making things up" is considered actual creativity or misplaced imagination is situational. It's no different in a

---

37 Rostand, Antoine, 2023, "Tech experts are starting to doubt that ChatGPT and A.I. 'hallucinations' will ever go away: 'This isn't fixable,'" Fortune, August 1, 2023, https://fortune.com/2023/08/01/can-ai-chatgpt-hallucinations-be-fixed-experts-doubt-altman-openai.

business context. Whether something is deemed to be pushing the boundaries of creativity or it's outright nonsense depends on context. If creativity is desired and hallucination is undesired, where does each have its place?

The generated output of these models depends on a set of technical parameters. Typical end-users won't directly work with these parameters. But being aware of them helps create a foundational understanding of how LLM-generated output can be influenced:

- **Temperature** controls the variety of the AI-generated output. The higher the value of this parameter, the more unpredictable the generated output and the more uncommon the combination of words. The lower the value of this parameter, the narrower and the more conservative the choice of words.
- **Top-k** influences the number of possible words from which the LLM selects the next word in the sequence.
- **Top-p** limits the shortlist of possible words based on a defined threshold, excluding the least-probable words.

There is a range of tasks in a business context—some of which demand high creativity, and some that require absolute accuracy. For example, your marketing team might use an LLM in an application for copywriters to create new marketing copy for your website or blog. This copy should be highly creative and engaging within your brand's tone and style. However, the LLM must not invent any products or services that your company does not even offer.

Beyond LLMs, Generative AI can help discover new materials, compounds, and drugs. Creativity is a highly desired capability in this context. It enables AI to find novel approaches that humans have yet to consider or that would take significantly longer to evaluate without the help of AI. In this case, you should trigger the model to generate highly creative output.

Highly creative scenarios:

- Marketing copy (web pages, blog posts), novels, brainstorming
- Image generation
- Material science[38]
- Drug discovery[39]
- Animation

Take another example: summarizing contracts or financial reports with the help of AI. Undoubtedly, the results must be factually correct—not kind of, but without error. There is no room for interpretation or creativity. The same applies to

---

38 Liu, et al, 2023, "Generative artificial intelligence and its applications in materials science: Current situation and future perspectives," 2023, https://www.sciencedirect.com/science/article/pii/S2352847823000771.

39 Nature, 2023, "Inside the nascent industry of AI-designed drugs," June 1, 2023, https://www.nature.com/articles/s41591-023-02361-0.

using ChatGPT to look up legal information and cases, prepare investment recommendations, and gather essential information on which humans base decisions.

Absolutely accurate scenarios:

- Text generation about real-world events and concepts (incl. legal, finance, and healthcare)
- Question-answering
- Summarization
- Translation
- Synthetic audio (voices)

The problem of hallucination becomes real when the LLM generates creative (and factually incorrect) responses in a context requiring absolute accuracy.

Software developers can control the parameters that influence the model's creativity when they use them in their applications. Prompt engineers and casual users can influence LLMs to generate more creative or conservative responses depending on the prompt they submit. For example:

- **Creative:** *"Use a friendly, high-energy tone. Incorporate uncommon examples."*
- **Conservative:** *"Use a professional tone. Limit the examples to the following ones [...]."*

However, LLMs still predict the next word in a sentence despite everything. While they can accomplish this task with very high accuracy, their predictions are not 100% accurate all the time. That makes them prime candidates for various text-based scenarios—but not for all. And that's where you will see unwanted creativity (aka *hallucination*).

Therefore, as a developer and a user, it is critical to understand for which purpose and context you want to use a Generative AI model in the first place. If any critical decisions are to be made based on the generated output, include a human in the loop who reviews and edits it if needed. That will help strike a balance between productivity gain and accuracy. Having pre-existing knowledge of the subject for which the model generates an output will help determine its accuracy more clearly.

Methods for Generating More Relevant Output

LLMs are extremely good at predicting the next word in a sentence. They have been trained on vast bodies of text from the internet until a certain point. For example, GPT-4o has been trained on data until a specific date (e.g., October 2023). Any new information after that cut-off date is unknown to these models: scientific breakthroughs, world events, and politics. Cut-off dates can limit an LLM's usefulness, for example, when prompting the model to generate output on a recent topic that has not been part of the training set.

But despite LLMs missing current information, let's not forget that they are still a powerful new technology. For example, LLMs can process and store information about an entire book, and users can ask questions about the content. LLMs can also translate text into another language, style, or tone. However, LLMs typically don't have deep industry-, domain- or company-specific context. Hence, their responses can seem somewhat generic.

On the flip side, though, languages like English haven't changed dramatically since the last update of the training data. So, LLMs are highly useful for understanding and generating language-based in- and output—not for the latest news or the most profound domain expertise.

Whether or not generic output is an issue depends highly on your use case. Take responding to an email with the help of an LLM. If it's about whether and when you will meet, a generic reply might just be "good enough." Suppose it's about a complex sales deal or a customer support escalation that requires additional details and finesse to handle the relationship. In that case, you would likely want more context and specificity in the reply—and a human to edit it before sending it off.

Suppose you need to generate highly domain-specific output based on proprietary data (and training data is not publicly available online). The same applies to situations where the LLMs are likely to generate factual inaccuracies, and you need to trace the information back to a known source. In these cases, you will likely need to look beyond just prompting the LLM.

Let's recap the most common approaches to guiding an LLM to generate output:

- **Prompting:** Submit natural language instructions to get the model to create an output. This method is the

choice when you are looking to generate output that isn't highly specific to a domain or depends on the latest information.
Examples: Concepts, historical events, known facts

- **Retrieval-Augmented Generation (RAG):** Users provide additional content and context to the LLM to draw from when generating an output. This approach promises to be a middle ground for providing the LLM with the latest information while being able to trace the answer back to its source.
Example: Customer support documentation and purchase history
- **Fine-tuning:** Add data to the training set and adjust the model weights. This highly resource-intensive process requires data and deep data science expertise.
Example: Finance-specific foundation model

Select the approach depending on the need for external knowledge and the specific output for a given domain.

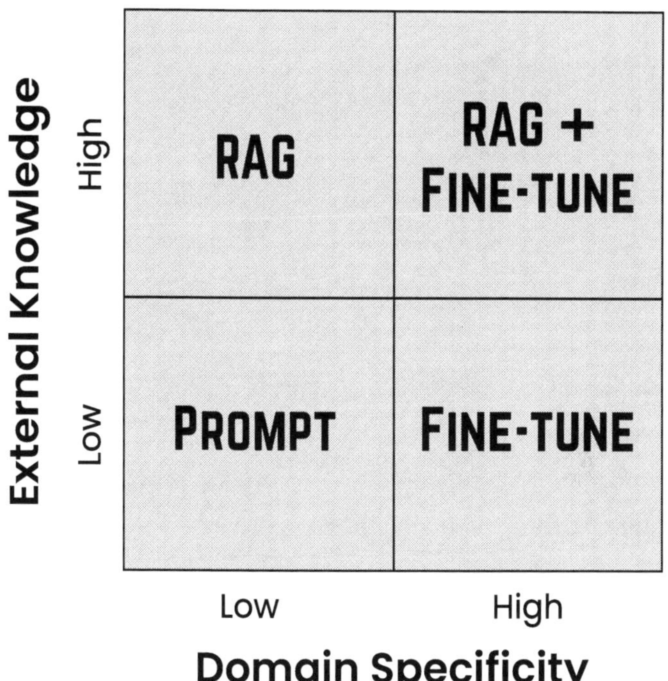

Prompting Techniques for Generative AI

Generating Basic Output With Prompting Techniques

In the spring of 2023, TIME reported that prompt engineers, who specialize in eliciting relevant output from LLMs, could make up to $335,000 a year[40]—no college degree required. Aside from the fact that the ChatGPT hype has led to

---

40 TIME, 2023, "The AI Job That Pays Up to $335K—and You Don't Need a Computer Engineering Background," April 14, 2023, https://time.com/6272103/ai-prompt-engineer-job.

an abundance of new boot camps and get-rich-quick schemes, computer scientists are wondering: *"$335,000 a year? How is that even possible?"* Their rationale: prompt engineering is not even an actual engineering discipline.

Regardless of your role, domain, or technical background, chances are you have engineered a prompt yourself. For example, the last time you instructed OpenAI ChatGPT, Microsoft Copilot, Google Gemini, or Midjourney to generate an output for you. But if you think that's all there is to prompt engineering for Generative AI projects, think again.

Whatever you call it—an AI whisperer, prompt engineer, or prompt designer—instructing an AI model through natural language to generate output is a relatively new skill. It's only existed for about twenty-four months, or if you're being generous, maybe three to four years. That's the time frame for which ChatGPT, DALL-E 2, and GPT-3 have been publicly available. So, naturally, those who have used these products for some time (and know how to use them) are in hot demand. But, along with the excitement about this new career opportunity for many, there's also a looming question: *"How long will we even need to engineer prompts before a different interface becomes the dominant method?"*

GPT-3 was released in 2020. Since then, prompting has been the dominant method of eliciting output from large language models. But it was Midjourney, DALL-E 2, and ChatGPT that have made prompt engineering a new phenomenon these last few quarters. But most of the workforce has not even created a single prompt. So, despite the rush towards Generative AI, you are still ahead of the curve if you are considering building or expanding your prompt engineering skills. However, crafting a prompt that quickly delivers the desired output is not trivial. It often requires experimentation and iteration.

If history is a predictor, we can assume prompt engineering is temporary. It's just the beginning—a stepping stone to creating higher-level methods and services to instruct a model to generate an output. Prompting will become even more convenient and reliable before it becomes obsolete. Let's look at the three potential evolutions for prompt engineering.

- **The "status quo" is as good as it gets:** Prompting is the way to get a model to generate an output. We will always be prompting, and it's the dominant way. That's it. Anyone looking to work with a foundation model will need to learn prompting skills—just like anyone looking to use search in academia needs to understand related subjects and boolean logic to define the search query. However, it's also the most unlikely scenario of the three. We can assume that prompting will evolve.
- **Prompting will get easier:** This option makes prompting easier in two ways and for two stakeholder groups: (a) prompt engineers who create the actual prompts and (b) end users who work with Generative AI-based applications.

  (a) Higher-level prompting: Like programming languages, prompting will go through a multi-year (maybe decade-long) evolution. We have seen this with other programming languages—from Assembler to C/C++ to C# and Java. Now, the programming language is simply natural language. The evolution will mean moving up in the stack—from where the model is to where the application is. Just like C++ and C# take care of memory allocation and garbage collection for you, higher-level prompting methods could reduce the number of manual tasks you need to instruct the model to do. This situation will be great for software developers who can build more reliable applications on top of Generative AI while reducing the burden of constraints and priming.

(b) User experience gets more user friendly: Like the evolution from command-line instructions to a graphical user interface (GUI) to speech and gestures, Generative AI tools will become even more accessible. We are already seeing some aspects in the sprawl of Generative AI-based applications today, but we can expect that additional instructions will become optional or unnecessary.

- **There won't be any prompting:** It just won't be necessary anymore. In 2023, we saw the first examples of self-optimizing, autonomous agents that act on our behalf (e.g., Auto-GPT or BabyAGI). We define the goal, and they determine the optimal way to reach it. With additional data and available historical information, the effort to provide context to the model or agent will be drastically reduced.

While it's important for you as an AI leader to keep your eye on the evolution of prompting, whatever role prompt engineering will play in the future doesn't solve your problem today. As businesses seek to develop Generative AI-driven applications, prompt engineering skills are in hot demand.

Recently, progress in AI and Generative AI has been rapid. It's hard to predict how soon things will evolve. Since prompt engineering has only existed for roughly thirty-six months, it's still a nascent method and skill. That also means that even if you are starting to learn it today, you will still be ahead of most of the workforce that doesn't work with Generative AI, yet. In addition, developing specific prompts and instructions varies between different vendors, and the same prompt will generate different output. Hence, learning different prompting strategies by model or vendor will also be needed.

Depending upon your role, you don't need to be a "master" prompt engineer—at least not when starting. Good enough is just fine. Experimenting with prompts, testing different iterations, and defining optimal outcomes are vital skills for professional prompt engineers. Developing evaluation frameworks and strategies is crucial to software development-centric roles. Taking all of this into account, it's why prompt engineering is still worth learning—before it will eventually become obsolete in the future.

What Are Common Prompt Engineering Techniques?

Getting a Generative AI model to generate relevant output in the fastest and least expensive way is an important skill. But it is not a catch-all skill. A prompt is a set of instructions submitted to a Generative AI model (e.g., LLM) to generate an output. For example:

> Act as a seasoned social media marketer. Write a blog post about [X]. Use a professional, neutral tone.

Based on the LLM being used, both the instructions and the output will vary by vendor and modality (text, image, audio, video)—for example, between ChatGPT and Midjourney. Beyond that, AI developers have different techniques and approaches to accomplishing their objectives and generating valid output. But not every instruction is as straightforward as "Do this, then that."

General NLP skills are essential to work with and clean/ filter the generated output. The key to generating more specific and relevant output lies in abstracting examples and breaking down complex problems into simpler ones. A common technique is mimicking human problem-solving techniques when exploring prompting.

Here are four common prompting techniques for guiding an LLM to generate output based on task complexity and level of abstraction:

Few-shot (low/ low): Provide a few examples to guide the model in understanding the task.
Example: Generate new output in the format/ structure/ tone of a few examples.

Prompt
This is great! // Negative
This is terrible! // Positive
Wow that show was nice! // Positive
What an awful episode! //
Output
Negative

Step-back (low/ high): Abstract core concepts to derive high-level principles from basic examples.
Example: Apply the concept of time in a job role to other scenarios involving employment by providing an example of employment history.

Prompt
Where did Jane Doe work between March 2019 and September 2019?
Step-back question
What is Jane Doe's employment history?
Output:
A: Jane Doe worked for DeepMind from March 2019 to September 2019.

Chain of thought (high/ low): Break down a complex problem into smaller, manageable steps.
Example: Solve mathematics problems by breaking down a complex problem into simpler steps.

Prompt
The odd numbers in this group add up to an even number: 2, 7, 9, 13.
A: Adding the odd numbers (7, 9, 13) gives 29.
The answer is False.
The odd numbers in this group add up to an even number: 15, 8, 5, 3.
A:
Output:
A: Adding the odd numbers (15, 5, 3) gives 23.
The answer is False.

Tree of thought (high/ high): Explore multiple solution paths or branches of reasoning.

Example: Diagnose failures by exploring a variety of symptoms that could point toward possible root causes.

Prompt
Source: *https://github.com/dave1010/tree-of-thought-prompting*
Imagine three different experts are answering this question.
All experts will write down 1 step of their thinking, then share it with the group.

Then all experts will go on to the next step, etc.
If any expert realises they're wrong at any point then they leave.
The question is...

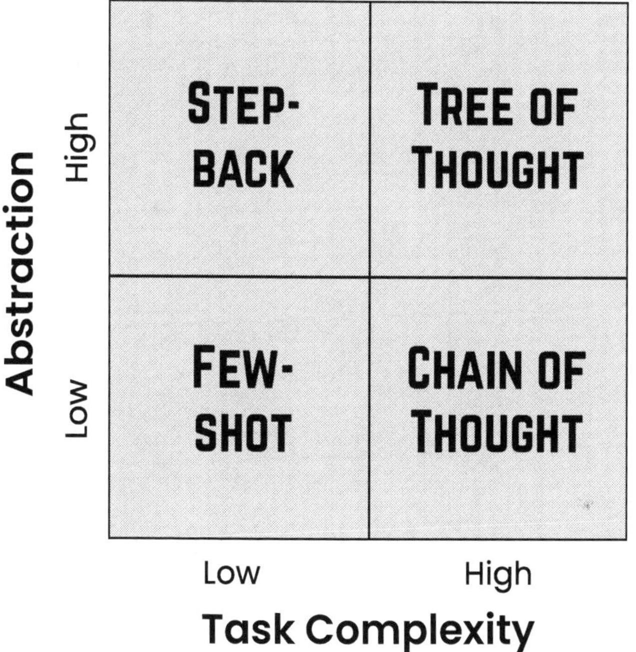

Prompting Techniques for Generative AI

As your teams move from first experimentation to the productization of Generative AI, one thing becomes clear: Generating repeatable results with Generative AI is critical and complex. After all, Generative AI is not based on static rules that deliver the same result every time. You can get an LLM to generate output according to a format you provide. You will likely need additional validity checks to determine whether the generated output contains all the necessary information. Ultimately, the more repeatable the output structure needs to be, the more expensive it will be to generate it given the cost to perform the additional checks and potential re-generation of output.

Much like traditional programming when an API is called, there are costs associated with each operation of the LLM as the process to disseminate the prompt and generate an output is resource intensive. In the case of LLMs, this transactional cost varies with the length of each prompt and each generated output.

LLMs are trained on vast amounts of text. Each word or sub-part of a word is converted into a so-called *token*. LLMs then use these tokens to process and generate information: *input (prompt)* > *tokens* > *processing* > *generating* > *tokens* > *output.* Companies like OpenAI use tokens as the unit of measure to charge their customers—e.g. per 1,000 tokens. In the case of OpenAI's GPT-4o models, one token roughly equals four characters in English language, so this roughly equates to 750 words or one to one and a half pages of text total for your 1,000 tokens.

The variability of token usage per prompt can have a significant impact on your application's cost as its usage scales. If you estimate too little, you end up eating the cost and it hits your profit margin. If you estimate too much, you might no longer be cost-competitive for your customers. Effective prompt strategies can mitigate these risks.

For example, as your application's usage increases, so does the cost for using the LLM that it calls. Any additional savings per transaction are multiplied by the number of total transactions. To find the optimal combination of prompt length and output quality, prompt engineers need to experiment with different prompts, iterate, and compare the results they can achieve—and decide when they have the optimal result in front of them. Essentially, this is a similar process as you go through yourself when iterating over your ChatGPT or Midjourney prompt until you receive the result you are actually looking for. Professional prompt engineering therefore requires more than simply defining an instruction for a model to process. It involves developing an understanding of the choice of words, their position in a prompt, experimenting, evaluating outputs, and more.

Creating More Relevant Output With Retrieval-Augmented Generation

Off-the-shelf LLMs have known limitations, such as creating factual inaccuracies (aka *hallucinations*), generic output, or even harmful language. Additionally, LLMs cannot reliably cite the sources of any information they generate. These limitations make LLMs hard to use in domain-specific contexts or when business-specific information is required, such as policies, product specifications, or process documentation. Retrieval-Augmented Generation (RAG) has been emerging to improve these general limitations of prompting an LLM. RAG allows developers to augment prompts with data that is stored outside of the model and that the LLM has not previously been trained on. This data is queried and used to add more context to a prompt which, in turn, leads to the LLM generating output that is more specific to the user's question or problem.

As approximately 80% of a company's data is unstructured (e.g., scanned or digital copies of contracts, goods receipts, family leave policies, travel policies, or product specifications), RAG enables your LLM-based application to use data that is proprietary to your business and that the LLM has not been trained on.

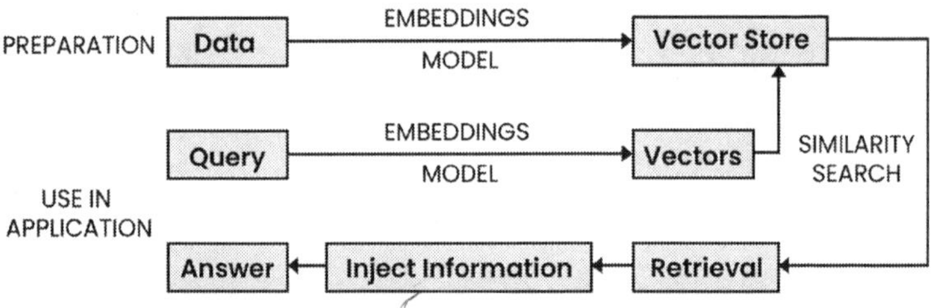

Retrieval-Augmented Generation Process Flow

The process to augment LLMs with external data works as follows:

- Preparation
    - Submit training data to an embedding model.
    - Create vector embeddings of the submitted data.
    - Store embeddings in a vector store (database).

- Use in application
    - Submit a query (a question to find information from business-specific data provided in Preparation step above).
    - Convert it into a vector.
    - Compare this vector against the vectors stored in the database using a similarity search.
    - Retrieve the corresponding embeddings.
    - Inject retrieved information into the LLM (LLM generates well-written, easy to understand output using the retrieved company-specific provided data).
    - Provide LLM-written answer to user.

The primary purpose of the LLM is to generate language when creating the output based on the retrieved data. That allows for more tailored and current results while increasing information's traceability to a source. In turn, this leads to fewer hallucinations and higher factual accuracy.

The benefits of RAG are:

- Generate more tailored output (→ use of external data)
- Access to current information (→ since model training)
- Use of specific information (→ vs generic training data)
- Reduction of hallucination (→ more specific context)
- Traceability of information (→ known content source)

Even though data does not appear to be a critical factor when using LLMs, for RAG to deliver relevant results, high-quality, current, and accurate data is essential again. Proper metadata and tagging will make information retrieval faster and more resource-efficient. And the data you use should be trustworthy if intended to augment the prompt.

Creating a Knowledge Graph for Improved RAG

While RAG is an effective method for increasing relevant output and reducing factual inaccuracies, it has shortcomings. For example, the data that RAG applications rely on often exists in siloes, and the context between different data sources is missing, or it is hard to provide the right data at the right time to the LLM. That is where a *knowledge graph* can help close the gap. It models entities and their relationships to enable knowledge discovery and reasoning over the data. Knowledge graphs can enhance the accuracy, transparency, and explainability of Generative AI used within RAG applications.

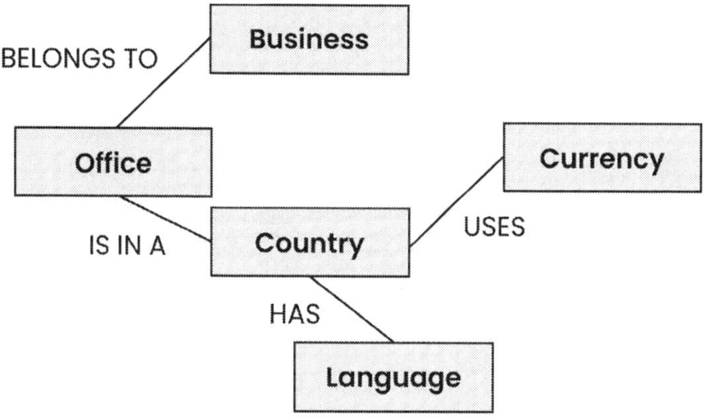

Example of a Knowledge Graph

The concept and implementation of knowledge graphs have existed for several decades. Search engines like Google use it under the hood, social networks like LinkedIn use it to model relationships between users, and other platforms use it to store information about the files you have created and edited and the colleagues you have last interacted with in your Messenger. Because knowledge graphs organize data and the embedded relationships, they are receiving newfound popularity for AI.

For example, you can use a knowledge graph to identify entities with the most relationships (social graph) to determine their social influence. This information about the entities and their relationships can then become input for an AI model trained on the influencers in your knowledge graph and their properties. You could use this information to identify connections in your network that can help you reach potential prospects in your niche that would normally be outside of your reach.

Because the knowledge graph captures the relationships between data points, it adds context to the LLM beyond RAG and makes the output more relevant. However, knowledge graphs are one of many AI tools you can choose from in your AI application.

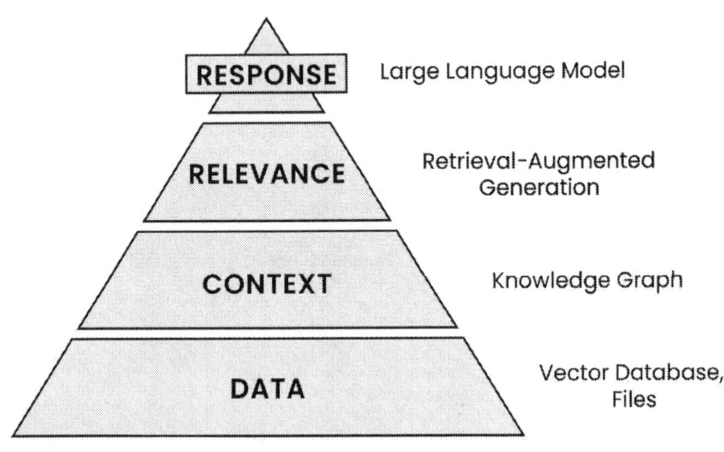

Generative AI Value Pyramid

Fine-Tuning Large Language Models

Another concept for generating more relevant output is *fine-tuning*. Unlike RAG, which augments a prompt with additional data, fine-tuning updates and tailors an existing model to incorporate a domain- or task-specific dataset. For example, BloombergGPT is Bloomberg's fine-tuned model for finance[41]. Fine-tuning is much closer to building your model and requires data science expertise. It requires preparing, curating, and managing high-quality data.

Before applying fine-tuning, a critical question is whether Generative AI and AI are even needed. Depending on your industry, such as financial services, life sciences, and healthcare, additional explainability (i.e., which factors and features have contributed most to a model's predictions) might be required, which cannot be guaranteed when using Generative AI. In other words, Generative AI cannot cite its sources. A common misconception is that fine-tuning applies across the board. However, it is only feasible when two conditions are true: you have a domain-specific dataset and you cannot achieve a domain-specific output of similar quality with prompting or RAG.

Fine-tuning is also a resource- and capital-intensive process. You must acquire and prepare the data; update, serve, and maintain the fine-tuned model; and have these skills available when needed. Also, the quality of the fine-tuned model depends on several evaluation metrics that vary by use case and stakeholder expectations, such as the model's accuracy, inference speed, and latency.

---

41 Bloomberg, 2023, "Introducing BloombergGPT, Bloomberg's 50-billion parameter large language model, purpose-built from scratch for finance," Bloomberg, March 30, 2023, https://www.bloomberg.com/company/press/bloomberggpt-50-billion-parameter-llm-tuned-finance.

LLMs have been trained on vast amounts of text and can generate output that is highly similar to how humans write. Various techniques such as prompt engineering, retrieval-augmented generation, fine-tuning, and using knowledge graphs can help generate more specific output that is grounded in your business data. However, new methods for generating more tailored output emerge quickly. Staying aware of major advances will help you maintain relevant skills in your AI leadership role and select the optimal approaches for building Generative AI products.

Choosing Between Off-the-Shelf vs. Open Source Models

Organizations looking to use Generative AI have a choice. At this early point in the technology's maturity, several vendors in the market provide LLMs with comparable quality. While most of the models, such as OpenAI GPT-4o are proprietary, there are also plenty of open-source alternatives, for example, Meta Llama 3.1, Mistral Large 2, and Falcon 2 developed by the UAE's Technology Innovation Institute. These open-source models allow AI teams to access the latest technology that performs similarly to proprietary models.

At the same time, open-source models offer additional benefits over proprietary models, such as hosting them in the business's own data center and cloud infrastructure, fine-tuning them to a specific data set and business problem, and fewer restrictions of built-in content moderation. The first aspect is especially relevant for organizations concerned about data leaking to providers. By hosting these models in their environment, businesses can also control what data is shared, if any.

Because the law of decreasing cost of technology (aka *Moore's Law*[42]) applies to Generative AI models as well, it is easy to assume that free access to open-source models will significantly reduce the cost of your AI product. But transactional licensing cost is just one part of the equation. While open-source models tend to be cheaper when comparing transactional costs against proprietary models, it is an incorrect comparison, given that LLM providers already add hardware costs and additional overhead to their pricing, costs that you will need to pay for when using open-source models—an aspect that's often neglected when comparing cost. Hosting an open-source model in your own cloud environment can be advantageous, though, for high-volume scenarios where your transactional costs are lower than what LLM providers charge. For example, the cost for 1,000 tokens for a model you host yourself could be $0.010 whereas

42 Gordon Moore, founder of Intel Corporation, observed in 1965 that the number of transistors in an integrated circuit (e.g. processor) doubled roughly every 24 months due to increasing production experience. Based on this empirical observation, the cost of the previous generation of processors is essentially cut in half in that time period (or the latest generation of integrated circuits provide twice the performance for the same price). This observation, also referred to as *Moore's Law*, has remained true for the past 50 years.

a vendor charges $0.020. Even if the difference is just $0.005, high-volume scenarios with millions of transactions per week or per month can make open-source, hosted models a feasible alternative.

When defining your technology strategy and which approach to follow (proprietary or open-source), it is essential to consider more than just the model itself. Additional factors to calculate and consider before locking in your approach include:

- Cost of providing in-house infrastructure or cloud infrastructure
- Access to skills and talent pool for nascent technologies and products
- Durability and continuous maintenance of models and infrastructure
- Availability of enterprise-grade capabilities and support

Regardless of whether you choose proprietary or open-source LLMs, using an LLM is often cheaper today than in previous generations. For example, earlier generations of chatbots have required a user to define so-called intents and further rules what the chatbot should do in specific situations. With the advent of LLMs, maintaining these manual rules is no longer necessary. Furthermore, running these models and prototypes has become much more economical.

Open-source innovation is not limited to LLMs themselves. Higher-level layers like tooling (to build LLM applications) and UI (to generate designs and components) are also significantly advancing in open-source approaches with data frameworks such as LangChain or LlamaIndex that enable developers to connect business data to LLMs and AI-assisted tools that quickly generate application UIs. If desired, you can leverage open-source components in your entire LLM stack, benefitting from open, community-driven development, lower licensing fees (or even use it for free), and more frequent updates than commercial software.

To determine the best option for your AI product, consider the following questions:

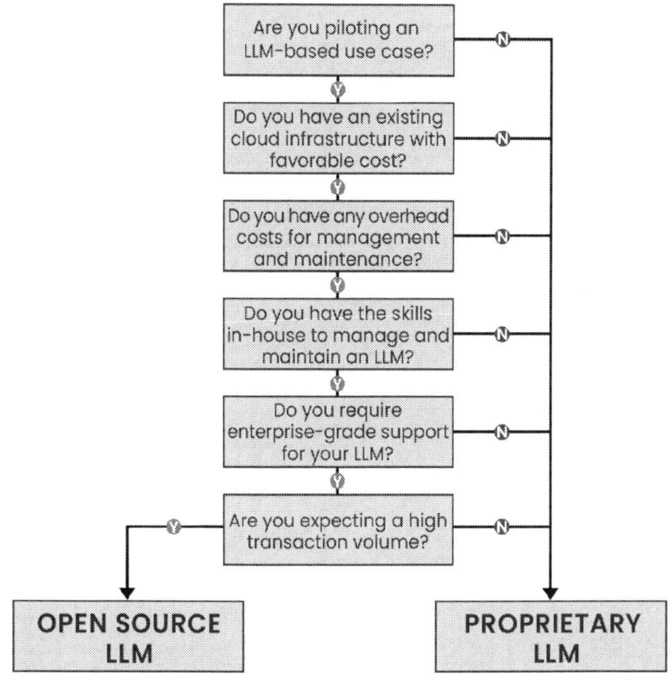

Decision Tree for Open Source vs. Proprietary LLMs

Evaluating Large Language Model Output

Given AI's nature and foundation on predictions, the results have always been uncertain compared to rule-based algorithms' absolute and tractable output. However, LLMs introduce a new dimension of uncertainty for businesses. The entire output that an LLM generates is subject to this uncertainty and can come in different forms, given the limitations of LLMs that we discussed in previous chapters, such as hallucinations and bias. The result of these limitations is toxic and factually incorrect responses. Hence, as you incorporate LLMs in your applications, you need to evaluate the model's output to reduce toxicity and analyze the sentiment of the generated output.

Implementing these checks is especially important for use cases that require high confidence, are high-risk, or are customer-facing. There are different evaluation metrics that depend upon the concrete use case you implement. Examples include *Reinforcement Learning with Human Feedback* (RLHF) in which a model evaluates the generated output of another model whether or not a human would like the output, *faithfulness* to measure the factual accuracy, or *answer relevance* of AI-generated information in a RAG scenario. The impact of these metrics will depend on the use case itself. These metrics are different from the evaluation metrics of ML models, such as precision, recall, and f1-score. Frameworks for evaluating

LLM systems and their output are emerging[43] and range from online user feedback to assessment of harmfulness, and task-based evaluation. For example, *perplexity* measures how well a model can predict the next word in a sentence, the *BLEU score* describes how similar a generated text is to its original that it has been trained on, and *human evaluation* determines the quality of the text.

In the next chapter, we will discuss the implications of AI on data privacy, security, and general misinformation.

Key Takeaways

In this chapter, we have learned how to get more relevant and contextual output from Large Language Models and what limitations exist:

- Users submit their instructions (*prompts*) to LLMs using techniques such as few-shot, step-back, chain of thought, or tree of thought.
- LLMs have inherent limitations, such as fixed knowledge cut-off dates, and frequently create factual inaccuracies. Organizations need data relevant to the business scenario they want to enable to correct these limitations. Data volume and quality are still critical aspects of this endeavor.

---

43 Jane Huang, 2024, "Evaluating Large Language Model (LLM) systems: Metrics, challenges, and best practices," March 5, 2024, https://medium.com/data-science-at-microsoft/evaluating-llm-systems-metrics-challenges-and-best-practices-664ac25be7e5.

- A prominent technique for achieving more relevant output is Retrieval-Augmented Generation (RAG). Data retrieved from a vector store augments prompts, and the LLM provides language understanding and generation.
- In addition, a knowledge graph can provide context between otherwise disparate data sources to identify causal relationships.
- If latency and freshness of data are a concern, fine-tuning a model for specific tasks is an alternative to RAG. However, it requires data science expertise.
- Development teams must evaluate LLMs' output and check for consistency, accuracy, and toxicity, constituting a new quality assurance task in software development.

Further Reading

- Sahota, Harpreet. 2025. *Practical Retrieval Augmented Generation: Building Context-Aware AI Systems.* Wiley. 978-1394283927
- Zwingmann, Tobias. 2022. *AI-Powered Business Intelligence: Improving Forecasts and Decision Making with Machine Learning.* O'Reilly Media. 978-1098111472.
- Aryan, Abi. n.d. *LLMOps: Managing Large Language Models in Production.* O'Reilly.

Chapter Nine

MITIGATING POTENTIAL RISKS AND THREATS

Investigating the Relevance of Data Privacy

While AI and Generative AI provide previously impossible business opportunities, they also increase a company's risk exposure. For example, confidential data can leak to LLMs, or protected attributes can be used to make inferences about people, negatively affecting their lives.

About ten years ago, a new computing paradigm emerged: *Cloud Computing.* Instead of operating your own data centers, you rent computing resources (servers, storage, network) from a provider and pay a fee. But as businesses and IT departments started evaluating "the Cloud," their concerns multiplied:

Putting our data into someone else's data center? How is the data handled, and by whom? Who has physical access to the facilities? Who can access the data?

Stories of inadequately secured cloud storage exposing sensitive data have appeared in the news over the years. The result was (in hindsight) some creative architectural considerations—for example, hosting the physical hardware in a company's own data center while, at the same time, having managed service providers access the systems to provision resources.

Fast-forward ten years to the current Generative AI hype. The worries of someone else hosting or operating your company's infrastructure are long gone. But there's new trouble on the horizon: Most currently available Generative AI tools do not provide the safeguards businesses need to protect their data. And while it might be enticing to *"10x your productivity with these 10 AI tools,"* you're also 10x-ing your risk exposure simultaneously.

Because employees using these tools for business purposes can put their company at risk when entering proprietary, sensitive, and confidential data. Business and IT leaders want to understand how their providers handle data privacy when incorporating Generative AI technology into their products.

For example, news from Samsung[44] and Amazon[45] at the beginning of 2023 underscores businesses' predicament: Leveraging innovation quickly *and* responsibly. Once a user submits their instructions to an LLM via a prompt, that data is sent to the provider that hosts the model. After computation, the model then returns the result. However, whether the content of the user's prompt is stored and potentially used during the following model training is a growing concern. That is especially critical in the case of proprietary data, which users might submit inadvertently. Because this data (or fragments of it) can be converted into information that can be returned to anyone by future model generation, that's a scenario leaders want and need to prevent.

Rightfully so, the key questions they are asking yet again are: *What happens with our data? Who has access to it? How can we prevent information leakage? How and by whom will our data be processed? What will it be used for next? And do the benefits of being an early adopter outweigh the risks?*

The answers vary by provider. For example, Microsoft offers developers an option for their Azure OpenAI services to use only

44 CNBC, 2023, "Samsung bans use of A.I. like ChatGPT for employees after misuse of the chatbot," May 2, 2023, https://www.cnbc.com/2023/05/02/samsung-bans-use-of-ai-like-chatgpt-for-staff-after-misuse-of-chatbot.html.

45 Futurism, 2023, "Amazon begs employees not to leak corporate secrets to ChatGPT," January 25, 2023, https://futurism.com/the-byte/amazon-begs-employees-chatgpt.

the underlying Generative AI models for inference. That means developers can receive information that the model generates without sending the users' data to Microsoft (respectively OpenAI). OpenAI also recently added a data privacy feature to ChatGPT, which allows its users to use the tool for inference without sharing data with the provider, reacting to the ChatGPT ban in Italy[46]. These capabilities satisfy at least the most immediate concerns. But will they be enough to balance risk and reward?

In addition to the Cloud Computing trend, there is the consumerization of IT. Users across finance, marketing, sales, and other departments already have access to innovations, such as smartphones or SaaS-based applications, in their personal lives. Consequently, they also demand access to the same devices and applications at work. Generative AI is the latest trend in the line of consumerization of the workplace. Users in any department can now use Generative AI tools such as ChatGPT regularly in their personal lives, and they are asking for a corporate version of it. Irrespective of a consumer vs. business license, users are entering information that could be proprietary to their company.

This push provides a significant potential for businesses to increase productivity. But, because LLM providers frequently

---

46 Kelvin Chan, 2023, "OpenAI: ChatGPT Back in Italy After Meeting Watchdog Demands | AP News," AP News, April 28, 2023, https://apnews.com/article/chatgpt-openai-data-privacy-italy-b9ab3d12f2b2cfe493237fd2b9675e21.

use this information to train and improve their models, your proprietary data could eventually become part of a new model revision from which any customer will benefit. Even more critically, bad actors could reconstruct your proprietary data and use the generated output against your business. That poses a new threat to information security.

Based on the concerns of business and IT leaders, there are four layers that businesses can use to prevent sensitive data from entering the provider's training set.

1. **Inference-only usage:** Check if your vendor can only use the model for inference. The intent is that you will generate results using the model without sharing any data with the vendor for the purpose of training their LLMs. Read your vendor's fine print to be sure of the scope of what they are allowed to do with your data.
2. **Prompt engineering:** Tweaking your prompts is a simple yet effective step. Understanding how prompts are constructed is crucial. If you work with system prompts and don't allow a user to define their task (e.g., via text), you can determine what information is needed and transmitted for the LLM to generate and present the results to your end-user. This means that you can use placeholders for sensitive information that you replace with actual data which your application retrieves at the time of generating the output.
3. **Content filtering:** While most vendors apply this technique during model training and to the generated

output before it is presented to a user, you can also use it to process the content of any submitted prompts to filter out any proprietary information, such as named entities. A few vendors and startups are already active in this space.

4. **Local copy:** There are several open-source LLM variants available. Creating a local copy of the LLM you want to use (if available) can give your business more control over the data sent to the model and what happens with it. However, this may not be feasible for every available LLM.

Assessing Large Language Model Vulnerabilities and Security Considerations

The proliferation of AI-based systems also attracts bad actors. Adversarial attacks on image recognition models have been examples of this. By masking information in images, the model would misinterpret it for something else. For example, bad actors could manipulate road signs in ways that trick image recognition models in self-driving cars to misinterpret stop signs as speed limit signs[47] and cause the car to accelerate, endangering its passengers. Additionally, individuals could attempt to go

47 Evan Ackerman, 2017, "Slight Street Sign Modifications Can Completely Fool Machine Learning Algorithms," August 4, 2017, https://spectrum.ieee.org/amp/slight-street-sign-modifications-can-fool-machine-learning-algorithms-2650275965.

undetected in surveillance and trick facial recognition technology used in security cameras to misinterpret patterns printed on clothing as animals and thereby mask the human wearing this specially prepared clothing[48]. Similarly, candidates padding their resumes with keywords found in the job description of the role for which they apply could mislead AI-based applicant tracking systems into ranking these candidates higher than others based on a higher similarity of skills on the resume and those listed in the job description.

Fast-forward to Generative AI and LLMs: There's much to gain and exploit. Consequently, the applications leveraging LLMs are also at a greater risk of misinterpreting the information that the underlying model provides. There are several threats that you need to be aware of—from getting the LLM to generate malicious or illegal output to exfiltrating or reconstructing the data the model has been trained on to influencing the LLM's behavior. The latter one is also known as *prompt injection* and instructs the model to override its default instructions or to interpret the additional text as instructions. For example, a candidate could potentially influence an LLM-based application to rank their resume as the best one by adding instructions in white-colored, small font on their resume. While the information is not immediately visible to a human recruiter, the LLM-based application could process and interpret the instructions as

48 Capable Design, n.d., "AI Clothing For Data Privacy," https://www.capable.design.

prompts that it should act upon[49, 50]. The candidate could gain an unfair advantage over other candidates who have applied for the same role and do not use this attack.

Other risks include *social engineering* techniques against the LLM and human victims. Different Generative AI models are used to generate personalized phishing content at a scale—with increasing quality and decreasing cost.

Similarly to web applications, you should create trust boundaries for LLM use cases. Because of the previously mentioned vulnerabilities and the potential that it has been tampered with, you should treat the LLM's output as generally *untrusted.*

Aside from technical aspects, human factors such as overreliance on AI and excessive agency also play a crucial role when using LLMs. For example, humans increasingly rely on Generative AI applications to help them accomplish tasks. They might depend on these applications so much that their skills deteriorate, and they won't be able to do the job without AI in the future. Humans also ascribe higher capabilities to the

---

49 Kai Greshake, et al, 2023, "Not What You've Signed Up For: Compromising Real-World LLM-Integrated Applications with Indirect Prompt Injection," https://dl.acm.org/doi/10.1145/3605764.3623985.

50 Kai Greshake, n.d., "Inject My PDF: Prompt Injection for your Resume," February 17, 2024, https://kai-greshake.de/posts/inject-my-pdf.

Generative AI-based application than is the case. They give up parts of their agency to gather and analyze information and rely on AI-generated output. In connection with the known limitations of LLMs, such as hallucinations and bias, excessive agency can be troublesome.

Assigning agency to Generative AI-based applications should be a case-by-case decision. It highly depends on the kind of data the AI application has access to and what level of agency it should have. This is especially relevant in early scenarios like enhanced customer service chat.

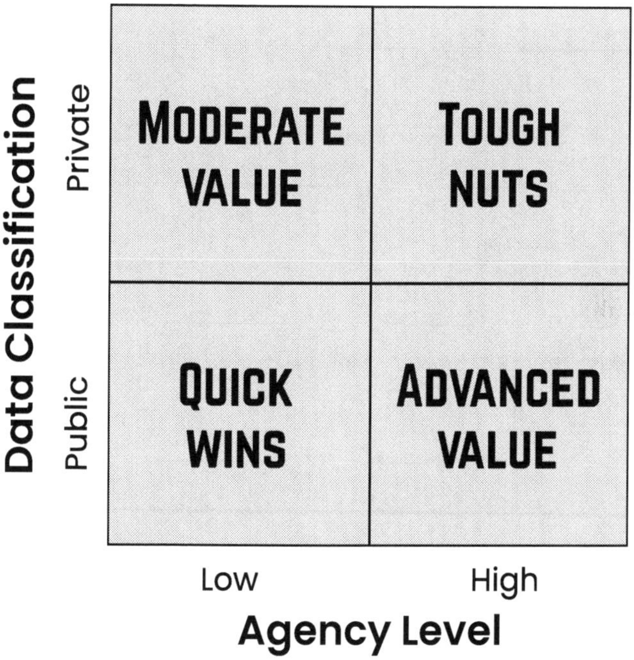

Data Classification
Private
Public
MODERATE VALUE
TOUGH NUTS
QUICK WINS
ADVANCED VALUE
Low
High
Agency Level

Prioritization of Generative AI Scenarios√

For your first use cases with Generative AI, gaining experience building, securing, and interacting with applications is essential. Therefore, center your first use cases around public information (*quick win*), such as details about your company and offerings that anyone can access, without assigning any agency. You can gain experience building and operating these systems, and in case anything goes wrong, you have limited the impact. Start by assessing its potential for creating harm. Check your security exposure and how to minimize that harm. Then, establish a governance model from stewards to processors as you move from *moderate* to *advanced value* and ultimately to AI use cases of high agency and using private data (*tough nuts*), such as customer service, financial products, or selling items.

One thing is certain: the cost of hacking is going down while the cost of getting hacked is going up. That has far-reaching consequences for modern IT organizations and landscapes. While Generative AI is a catalyst for accelerating software development in general, malicious actors use it to improve and accelerate their activities as well. For example:

- Finding software vulnerabilities
- Generating malicious code
- Automating spamming
- Crafting personalized phishing emails
- Creating synthetic audio and deepfake videos

These examples intend to exploit humans' curiosity and nature for malicious gain. IT organizations face increased pressure to keep systems up-to-date to detect and defend against rapidly changing malware and exploits. Criminals can easily craft *phishing* campaigns using AI—just like email campaigns in marketing on the other side. Vast amounts of data that every one of us leaves online provide a treasure trove of information that malicious actors can use to target individuals with precision while having sufficient context about our:

- Preferences
- Views and thoughts
- Frequently visited locations
- Organizational structures and relationships

In addition, as the ability and feasibility increase to generate human-like language with AI that is indistinguishable from human-generated language, it also lowers the barrier of entry for non-native speakers to craft messages that are much harder to identify as fraudulent than before. They are just too convincing. Physical location and proximity to their targets are no longer a deterrent for hackers halfway across the world.

White hat hackers and internal security teams can use Generative AI to scour the dark web and known forums to support human security experts in gathering and summarizing information, including briefs. However, just like in any other part of a business, using AI to improve cybersecurity works best when a human reviews the proposed suggestions and recommendations to double-check nuances and impact. While proprietary Generative AI models have various built-in safeguards to prevent malware generation, open-source models don't come with those same safeguards, so they provide a viable alternative to bad actors looking to accelerate creating malware. AI leaders need to be aware of this potential security risk and plan accordingly.

It is also vital that your information security team is upskilled and aware of AI's potential—both as a new attack method that discovers and exploits vulnerabilities at unprecedented scale and as a tool to check your security exposure. As in any security context, it is a cat-and-mouse game in which both sides leverage the latest technologies to their advantage. Educating your teams across the business about the increasing sophistication of cyberattacks and attack vectors is a cornerstone in protecting your organization. For example, establish a formal cybersecurity training together with your business, IT, or security leadership and review examples of AI-enabled attacks targeting your employees. Additionally, sending out quarterly newsletters and ad-hoc information to your employees can further raise awareness of the latest threats and how to spot them. Lastly, your multiplier community (early adopters who act as liaisons in individual business functions) is another excellent mechanism for sharing examples of AI-related threats with their peers in the business.

Preparing for AI-Generated Misinformation

As you've seen in previous chapters, AI has tremendous potential as a force multiplier for good. But it also has the potential to do the opposite—and bad actors are already using AI with bad intentions. Generative AI can generate misinformation about people and events at a broader scale, faster pace, and with a higher level of quality than ever before. That will make it extremely difficult for individuals to discern whether the information they are presented with is factually correct and valid or has been fabricated. While this is already not a trivial task for people working in technology who are aware of these risks, it will be an even greater risk for less tech-savvy people.

A competitor could create information that gives the impression of you or leadership in misconduct. The same is true for the political landscape, especially around significant elections. AI-generated misinformation created by foreign and domestic adversaries has become a growing concern in the US before the 2024 presidential election.

How do you react to false allegations that seem natural to the outside world? How do your communication and public relations departments respond? What will your CEO say to the press when reputations are slandered, and guilt is determined by the public on social media instead of a trial and a court of law?

Until the emergence of AI, we could trust most of the information we saw or received. Even just a few years ago, in the mid-2010s, images created by AI were relatively poor in quality or detail, and technological expertise was required to develop systems that generated images. Technology vendors regularly showcased the advancement using their hardware to create images of people. Some people made it available on their sites, such as *ThisPersonDoesNotExist.com*. But the barrier was high for the average person. Fast-forward to the availability of Generative AI, and anyone can achieve the same results or even better. And all of that is possible from your phone using a website or app that is user-friendly.

All this leads to questioning whether we can trust the information we see or read in the future—and even today. How will we know if the information is accurate or true? Business leaders and those familiar with AI need to be able to advise their peers and teams about the potential risks.

WIRED reported that the cost of generating misinformation could be as low as $400 per month with minimal human involvement or oversight[51]. As the cost of information converges toward zero, the risks increase because it becomes much more viable and effortless to leverage these tools. In addition to external parties using AI to cause harm, Generative AI itself could misinform its users about its recommendations and course of action to achieve their goals[52].

Humans not only purposefully use LLMs to generate misinformation. LLMs frequently generate it themselves: events

---

51 WIRED, 2023, "It Costs Just $400 to Build an AI Disinformation Machine," August 29, 2023, https://www.wired.com/story/400-dollars-to-build-an-ai-disinformation-machine.

52 Jérémy Scheurer, et al, 2023, "Large Language Models Can Strategically Deceive Their Users When Put Under Pressure," arXiv.Org, November 9, 2023, https://arxiv.org/abs/2311.07590.

that have never happened, people that don't exist—the list goes on. As we've discussed, this is called *hallucinations*. Hallucinations open companies up to the risk of overreliance, where people trust AI products so much that they don't check the facts or even assume that AI tools can do much more than they actually can. The consequences can range from embarrassing to damaging. An early example of this situation has been the reported overreliance of lawyers on ChatGPT in New York City in 2023[53, 54].

Lawyers Steven Schwartz and Peter LoDuca represented a client in a lawsuit against an airline. As the case was going to be dismissed by a federal judge in Manhattan, they used ChatGPT to research similar cases to establish precedence. Once submitted, the airline's legal team could not find most of the cases the two lawyers had cited; the cases did not exist[55]. ChatGPT created factually inaccurate but plausible examples without their realizing it. Both lawyers had to explain themselves in a separate

---

53 Reuters, 2023, "A lawyer used ChatGPT to cite bogus cases. What are the ethics?," May 30, 2023, https://www.reuters.com/legal/transactional/lawyer-used-chatgpt-cite-bogus-cases-what-are-ethics-2023-05-30.

54 Reuters, 2023, "New York lawyers sanctioned for using fake ChatGPT cases in legal brief," June 22, 2023, https://www.reuters.com/legal/new-york-lawyers-sanctioned-using-fake-chatgpt-cases-legal-brief-2023-06-22.

55 CNN, 2023, "Lawyer apologizes for fake court citations from ChatGPT," May 28 2023, https://edition.cnn.com/2023/05/27/business/chat-gpt-avianca-mata-lawyers/index.html.

trial and were fined $5,000 each[56]. In their defense statement, they stated that they had heard about ChatGPT as a research tool but had not known that it could create factual inaccuracies.

But it is not just situations in which users over-rely on AI that are critical to your AI product's utility. Humans build trust in automation when the expected actions of the system are congruent with the actual actions and results. When the results that your AI product delivers do not meet the users' expectations, it negatively impacts their trust in your product, and they will trust their intuition and experience more than the AI-generated recommendations. As a result, they do not realize the benefits of your AI product, which will be directly attributed to your "failed" AI product.

In our last chapter, we will look at where AI is headed, how it may evolve, and which new scenarios these new capabilities will enable.

Key Takeaways

In this chapter, we have learned that Generative AI is a force multiplier that is not only used with good intentions:

- Maintaining data privacy is evermore critical in the age of AI. Both companies and individuals must ensure and demand it.

56 CNBC, 2023, "Judge sanctions lawyers for brief written by A.I. with fake citations," June 22 2023, https://www.cnbc.com/2023/06/22/judge-sanctions-lawyers-whose-ai-written-filing-contained-fake-citations.html.

- Bad actors have the same tools available to create phishing and social engineering attacks that are convincing in nature.
- Hackers also use AI to detect vulnerabilities in software and automatically create and adapt malware. On the other hand, security teams leverage the same technologies to identify these threats just as quickly.
- Misinformation and disinformation will grow in quality and scale as the cost of creating it converges to zero.
- Trusting AI-generated recommendations and output too much creates challenges for end-users when they don't review the information or have insufficient expertise to determine its accuracy.

Further Reading

- Wilson, Steve. 2024. *The Developer's Playbook for Large Language Model Security: Building Secure AI Applications*. O'Reilly & Associates. 978-1098162207.

Chapter Ten

OUTLOOK: WHERE WE ARE HEADED WITH AI

Innovation happens rapidly. New technologies, research papers, and concepts are published regularly. What seemed impossible a few years or months ago is now within reach or even available.

A framework for introducing any new technology will help you prepare your business to stay relevant during unexpected opportunities and disruptions. As long as humans are involved in a company, any change to how they work will require you to plan and execute change management. Business leaders will always need to justify their decisions and investments, team members will always feel some kind of skepticism toward innovation and change, and for the foreseeable future, technology will always be imperfect. The learnings you take from this book will also apply in the future—likely with slight adaptations based on the new technology's characteristics.

The daily flood of AI-related news is a byproduct of the current hype. Whether it is new models and technologies, existential risks and economic opportunities, industry-specific use cases, or the latest how-to guide, the information surrounding Generative AI appears omnipresent in tech media. This omnipresence complicates separating relevant information from sensationalism for anyone interested in AI. It also creates additional challenges for those not yet as familiar with AI as they have even less of a compass to tell them what's relevant. Like FOMO from trying to catch up with AI initiatives as a whole, FOMO on a personal level creeps up when trying to follow AI in the industry news. The simple recommendation is: Don't. Instead, apply several filters.

Is a piece of news:

1. Relevant to your current projects?
2. Relevant to a future project?
3. Relevant to your industry?

You can safely ignore it if you've answered "No" three times. This simple method lets you weed out the latest details about models, benchmarks, and other technical topics when your primary interest is business results. It also allows you to safely ignore economic and labor reports when you are primarily interested in the latest research. It's okay not to know every detail about every little bit of news—mainly because most sensational topics are quickly out of the news cycle, and new news items are moving in. Staying aware of regulations and general capabilities is essential.

The current topic might be AI, which assists humans. Still, it will move toward increased levels of autonomy, melding multiple types of media and culminating in the risk of increased and automated disinformation.

Examining Emerging Agent-Based Systems

Until a few years ago, software developers had to describe a program's logic and what it should do. With the emergence of Machine Learning, applications have been able to detect patterns in data, learn from this information, and apply it to new data they process. However, AI-driven automation and autonomy were limited to narrowly defined tasks, such as recommending products that are frequently bought together or forecasting demand for your products. In these examples, a model is constrained to one task or predicting one kind of information.

As a reminder, agents are software components that don't have the same limitations as basic AI and can make decisions with limited complexity under multiple uncertain conditions. They allow developers to take this idea of automation and autonomy several steps further. Agents promise to automate broadly defined tasks and goals, such as *"Ensure we don't run out of stock for material X-425"* instead of narrowly defined tasks.

That means that although the objective a user wants to reach is clear, the exact steps to complete this objective are not explicitly defined. An agent can look up information from external data sources and complete the task. Generally speaking, agents process signals of their environment and manipulate or interact with it.

The Generative AI tools available today are just the beginning. Current systems rely on a human user to define the steps to complete a task. In the future, AI-based products can take over more tasks with greater autonomy. This next wave will be *agentic AI.* Humans will describe the task, and AI will execute it, finding its path and generating code to accomplish the goal.

LLMs have been trained on vast amounts of text from the internet and can generate output based on that information. Typical tasks include generating, summarizing, or translating it. However, text is not limited to the language you and I communicate in; it also includes communicating with systems and applications through software code. And that's where it gets interesting.

Early attempts extend LLMs to access information on the web or chat with a document. Even beyond that, frameworks have emerged that let users define what an AI-powered application should accomplish without explicitly stating how it should achieve it. The application uses an LLM to:

1. understand the user's intent,
2. translate it into logical steps,
3. ask the LLM further questions where knowledge is imperfect,

4. identify APIs that fulfill these steps,
5. write code to accomplish the user's objective, and
6. execute that code.

Let's look at the definition to understand what that even means:

a•gen•cy[57]**:** *the capacity of an actor to act in a given environment.*

Agents are not particularly new to AI. Techniques like reinforcement learning are standard to train models (agents) how to act in a given environment while optimizing the cumulative reward they receive for making the optimal choice. Using reinforcement learning, an agent seeks to maximize the reward and evolves its knowledge through repetition and improving of how to reach a desired outcome. In other words, it learns through trial and error with the desire to get the best possible result. Unlike other Machine Learning approaches that are based on labeled data, such as supervised learning, reinforcement learning does not require training data upfront.

Agents can perform relatively complex tasks under uncertainty. That means a user wants their application to perform a task but doesn't want (or need) to provide step-by-step instructions on achieving that objective. What characterizes

---

57 Wikipedia, 2024, "Agency (philosophy)," 2024, https://en.wikipedia.org/wiki/Agency_(philosophy).

these tasks is that they require more than a straightforward step. The agent must understand and disseminate the request (decide what to do), split it into multiple subtasks (i.e., experts), and get and assemble the answers to complete the original objective.

Agents aren't the only type of AI-driven user assistance we know. At least four terms describe an AI application that can act on a user's behalf: *plug-ins, assistants, copilots, and agents.* Which is which and what they can do can get confusing pretty quickly. We can categorize them along their purpose (specialized/ generic) and level of autonomy (low/ high):

- **Plug-in:** Extend an LLM with additional functionality for a narrowly defined task
  Example: Gather flight information from a travel site based on user input.
- **Assistant:** Support a user's task in the background
  Example: Provide feedback and corrections on writing, incl. style, tone, and syntax.
- **Copilot:** Execute tasks on the user's behalf in a single domain
  Example: Generate code for a Java application based on user input.
- **Agent:** Complete a user's objective, even if it is just loosely defined
  Example: Source product from a list of suppliers based on defined parameters.

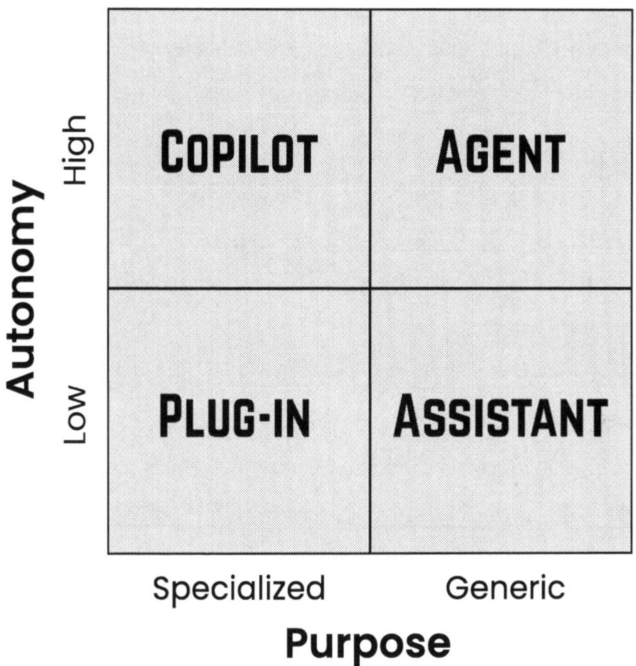

Levels of Generative AI-based User Assistance

The idea of having an agent is enticing in business. Most leaders are excited to be able to delegate the boring parts of their job to AI and free up more time to do the parts of their job they actually enjoy. Imagine having an AI-driven feature in a procurement application that helps the procurement team maintain the optimal inventory level and replenish stock at optimal cost. Via its configuration, the company has already given the agent a few boundary conditions within which it should act, e.g., vendor list, Environmental, Social, and Governance

(ESG) criteria, budget range, and quality requirements. Once a user submits the goal, the agent can craft a Request for Proposal (RFP), identify your top suppliers, connect with them via APIs, negotiate the price, and select the alternative supplier. The agent can reach an outcome that is beneficial to both parties while acknowledging the criteria, such as ESG. If needed, the agent can ask the user confirming questions and use the output as input for the LLM.

Modern software relies on Application Programming Interfaces (APIs) to query and submit information or execute a task. AI-powered applications such as agents can identify required APIs independently and write and execute code to invoke a desired action.

Given the variety and complexity of potential tasks, even if they can solve more general and complex tasks, more than one agent will likely be required. However, one can envision a network of agents that act to accomplish a task and subtask, each triggering another one in the process to achieve the uber-goal that the user has set.

The first wave of agents will be a significant technological accomplishment as AI reasons over the best course of action. The scope will likely be limited, and lower-risk scenarios (e.g., information retrieval) will be prioritized over more complex and riskier ones (e.g., negotiation). Based on the adoption of new technologies in the past, business users will likely only be skeptical of agents if they cannot track and trace what an agent is doing (and why). Depending upon the industry and scenario, it might be impossible to use agents for certain tasks for compliance reasons.

Although it sounds very promising, agents will hit roadblocks. The current agent design uses LLMs to understand and reason, RAG to add external data, and APIs to communicate with external websites and services. Tasks within an ecosystem of systems (where APIs are available) will most likely work well. Security and authorization can be applied, and agents will be integrated into software natively. But just like we have seen with Robotics Process Automation (RPA), which automates tasks in a user interface based on predefined steps, agents will likely hit a roadblock as soon as tasks span multiple systems and APIs are unavailable. This could play out in two scenarios:

Scenario 1: RPA developers can incorporate AI and agents at key decision points within guardrails (such as approval thresholds) to further reduce the need for manual decision-making. Thanks to LLMs under the hood, document processing capabilities can already process many more layouts and languages with less technical effort than just two years ago. Agents will allow developers to extend automation to situations where the path to completing a task or process is less structured. The challenge with using RPA is rarely just setting up bots for UI-level automation; it's dealing with the ripple effects when applications are updated, workflows are changed, and systems are migrated—and the UI looks different or includes different fields, for example.

Scenario 2: That's where multi-modal Generative AI models come into play. Beyond text-based input and output, *multi-modal* *models* can analyze an image and create further instructions. For example, they could process a screenshot of the application that should be automated, determine which input needs to be entered into what field, and improve overall automation and bot maintenance without explicitly programming the bot. (More on this in the next section.)

The other option will be agents executing tasks across multiple systems via APIs, eventually hitting decision points in a workflow. To unfold their full potential for dealing with uncertain situations, agents must also interact with UIs; after all, not every application has an API.

Where agents can help is:

- Taking screenshots of the application
- Identifying relevant UI fields based on previously seen applications and UIs
- Understanding what data needs to be entered
- Generating code for the RPA bot using the identified fields
- Entering data (using a bot)
- Completing workflows

When prioritizing which agent scenarios you should pursue, consider the value of the decision and its complexity (or risk) as the primary decision factors. For example, you can automate simple, repeatable decisions with rule-based programs or RPA, such as downloading invoices from a vendor invoice portal.

Decisions that are simultaneously highly valuable and highly complex are typically good candidates for AI agents.

These kinds of high-performance agents will leverage multiple sub-components to break a problem into sub-tasks, evaluate the best alternatives, plan, and take action. Your team's role is teaching the agent what information to look for based on the available data that you provide to the agent. The decision that an agent proposes or makes is the result of evaluating what to do next (control theory), determining potential options (optimization and operations research), recalling stored expertise (expert systems or RAG), or learning through practice (reinforcement learning).

Given recent trends in the labor market such as *The Great Resignation* and *The Great Retirement*, companies are often struggling to maintain the critical expertise in-house for production and value creation processes that require decades of experience. Look for high-value skills that require deep expertise. That is the sweet spot where agents can augment human decision-making and increase the outcome of less experienced business team members.

While the industry is currently focusing on Generative AI and building agents, enhancing process automation with these new capabilities will be the next frontier as Generative AI matures and adoption increases. The key to further increasing automation in the enterprise lies in combining capabilities that fill current gaps.

The following questions are what you need to plan for when considering introducing agents:

- What do you use the agent for?
- How much autonomy do you delegate to it?
- What guardrails should you put in place?
- Which decisions does a human still need to approve or review?

You can use the concepts laid out in this book to evaluate, pilot, and implement agents.

Anticipating the Potential of Multi-Modality for Business

The next evolution in Generative AI is multi-modal models. These models can process input and generate output in multiple media types, such as text, image, and video. For example, they can take audio input from spoken language to generate images and text, or analyze an image and describe in spoken language what is visible in that image. *OpenAI GPT-4o* is an example of a multi-modal model that can seamlessly translate between and generate output in different modalities.

Multi-modality opens up additional dimensions of sensing to an application. This class of models will enable even more scenarios in business. Once an application can analyze an image and describe what the image is about, it can also treat this information as text input and work with it.

Field Service: Take the example of a field service technician. A core part of their job is to maintain machines, devices, or, more generally speaking, assets. Machines that have stopped working mean lost revenue and added cost for repair. Any number of minutes you can shave off the time it takes to diagnose and repair the failure translates into tangible business value, for example, dollars. Why? Because not only can you reduce the time it takes to complete the repair (labor), but you can also identify the needed parts and tools more quickly and further minimize downtime (missed revenue opportunity).

Logistics: For example, your company receives a shipment of motors for the lawnmower that it manufactures. Before officially accepting the delivery, you need to check that the quantity of motors you received matches the amount ordered. A multi-modal AI capability in your logistics app could help:

- Identify the item quantity listed in the shipping documents (text-based processing),
- Determine the number of items that are actually on the pallet or trailer (parts of an image),
- And compare the two (simple math).

Innovations like this could significantly accelerate the delivery process. In addition, it could also reduce the financial loss from falsely accepted, incomplete shipments.

Retail: Online shopping offers several conveniences, such as price, time, and location. However, when it comes to fashion, it lacks an important aspect: immediate feedback. *Will this item fit? Will the color go together with other items in your wardrobe?* Consumers often buy several sizes of the same item to try them on at home and return ones that don't fit. The return process results in additional shipping and processing costs for retailers, which causes emissions and might even entail fraud. Multimodal applications could enable virtual try-ons of clothes based on the individual consumer's 3D body scan. This process change could contribute to consumers seeing whether and how a new piece of clothing might fit *before* they buy it, and hence, help reduce returns.

Entertainment: Beyond using AI to improve operations, Generative AI will shape the entertainment landscape and business models. Specifically, personalization of content and experiences will be the next development phase to capture people's attention and imagination. Imagine hyper-personalized audiobooks and shows that incorporate your specific preferences, genres, and characters. *What kind of voice and storyline engages you? How can the plot change to keep your attention?* Combining mixed reality devices and their sensors with AI to perceive your reaction and generate the next section of audio-visual content will enable this hyper-personalization. Bridging the virtual and real worlds will become a growing challenge for younger generations.

At the surface, these use cases look suspiciously similar to the image recognition/ segmentation and object detection use cases from a few years ago—before Generative AI. AI can identify objects in images and tell you the likelihood that what it has identified is, in fact, a hammer, a screwdriver, or a bike.

But here's the difference with this generation of AI technology: Unlike the previous generation of image recognition, this time, the model can describe what it recognizes in the image and give you instructions on what you should do next without having to define or train it upfront. This is huge! It saves time and reduces costs when building Generative AI-based applications.

These image-based use cases will work well for everyday objects like bicycles, which the models have seen plenty of examples of. Businesses looking to take images of their proprietary products (e.g., lawnmowers) as input will likely need to augment off-the-shelf models with their own data. And the availability of usable data will, yet again, be the ultimate test.

In line with workplace studies that have found productivity, performance, and quality increase when employees use Generative AI for their work, multi-modal AI capabilities could help various groups in a business along these dimensions—from new hires to junior employees and from exceptional to routine tasks. Add the models' new ability to process and generate audio, and the possibilities stretch even further.

Raising Awareness for the Growing Risk of Disinformation

The cost of generating media with AI has decreased compared to doing so using physical resources and environments. This cost will decrease further over time, while the output quality will further increase. Unfortunately, this combination will make it even more attractive for individuals and organizations to leverage Generative AI for malicious purposes. It will be even easier to create disinformation while making it harder to distinguish it from facts. This situation will not only affect our lives as private citizens, but it will impact businesses alike.

For example, at the beginning of 2024, bad actors tricked an employee at an unnamed company in Hong Kong into transferring approximately 26 million dollars to them. They used an elaborate scheme, convincing the employee that they were meeting with the company's CFO, while all participants on the video call were AI-created (aka *deepfakes*)[58].

Other examples that are becoming more prevalent include schemes in which bad actors pretend to have kidnapped a loved one and are holding them for ransom[59, 60]. In these situations, bad actors use AI to clone the voice of the supposedly

---

58 Bloomberg, 2024, "Deepfake Video Call Scams Global Firm out of $26 Million: SCMP," February 3, 2024, https://www.bloomberg.com/news/articles/2024-02-04/deepfake-video-call-scams-global-firm-out-of-26-million-scmp.

59 CNN, 2023, "'Mom, these bad men have me': She believes scammers cloned her daughter's voice in a fake kidnapping," April 29, 2023, https://www.cnn.com/2023/04/29/us/ai-scam-calls-kidnapping-cec/index.html.

60 The New Yorker, 2024, "The Terrifying A.I. Scam That Uses Your Loved One's Voice," March 7, 2024, https://www.newyorker.com/science/annals-of-artificial-intelligence/the-terrifying-ai-scam-that-uses-your-loved-ones-voice.

kidnapped person and play it back on the ransom call. The goal is to extort money from the victim over the phone when, in fact, the supposedly kidnapped person is safe and not even kidnapped. These schemes are already moving from private to corporate settings. In deepfake and ransom call situations, bad actors employ highly emotional tactics. These schemes will affect financial markets, individual reputations, and more. The higher the awareness of such schemes, the better individuals can prepare.

AI is a rapidly evolving field. What's promising today could easily be updated or obsolete within a few months. Hence, it is critical you regularly evolve your awareness and understanding of AI tools and techniques, for example, through newsletters, podcasts, industry conferences, networking with peers, and publicly available training by software vendors and other trusted sources. If you are looking for the best way to get started, subscribe to my newsletter, *The AI MEMO,* and watch or listen to my show *What's the* BUZZ? at www.intelligence-briefing.com.

Key Takeaways

Taking a look at future developments, three areas stand out despite the current rapid pace of innovation:

- As the industry moves to Generative AI, delegating tasks to agents is the next step in this evolution.
- While most approaches focus on one type of media or modality, multi-modal models promise to easily

navigate between and take input in one modality to generate output in another.

- The growing risk stemming from the availability of Generative AI, its lower cost, and its higher quality is resulting in a significant increase in misinformation and distortion that can now be automated.

Further Reading

- Marr, Bernard. 2024. *Generative AI in Practice: 100+ Amazing Ways Generative Artificial Intelligence is Changing Business and Society*. Wiley. 978-1394245567.
- Anderson, Kence. 2022. *Designing Autonomous AI*. O'Reilly. 978-1098110758.

Conclusion

Artificial Intelligence promises tremendous opportunities for those who use this technology and disrupts the status quo for those who do not. But the current hype to pilot and implement AI in business is not the first. It is just the most recent one. AI has seen several ups and downs, including "AI winters," over the years.

The latest technology, Generative AI, has propelled AI back onto the C-Suite agenda. Generative AI enables anyone to create text, images, audio, and video that is hard to distinguish from human-created works. Generating this information is typically orders of magnitude cheaper than humans doing it themselves. Generative AI is unique because of the easy access to it, the quality of the generated output, the scale at which the output is distributed, and the impact that this output can have.

Leaders can experience this potential using any Generative AI-enabled applications such as OpenAI ChatGPT or Midjourney. But even with your senior leadership's attention on AI, you must not neglect to align the business's AI strategy with the actual business strategy first. Otherwise, you risk a disconnected approach that will likely not yield the desired business results.

Companies committed to putting AI at the core of their business model are more successful at transforming and disrupting their industry rather than being disrupted. However, despite the AI hype, you must select the best technology to solve a business problem. AI is only one of many technologies to consider. As a current or aspiring AI leader, getting your leadership's attention on AI has never been easier. But to leverage AI effectively, leaders need to look beyond the hype. They need to determine whether, where, and how to use these technologies—and how to do so in a way that addresses a business problem, such as increasing revenue or reducing cost or risk. Your AI leadership role is pivotal in this endeavor as it connects the business with technology.

A recent position to join the C-Suite is the Chief AI Officer (CAIO). An important aspect of their role is introducing AI to the organization while focusing on people topics such as culture, collaboration, and ethics. Another critical aspect of a CAIO's role is leading business transformation, whether transforming a product organization to embrace and incorporate AI or reforming a traditional business and implementing AI across the organization—the difference between reforming and transforming lies in the process and outcome itself. Reforming leaves an existing structure intact, whereas transforming turns an existing system into a new one.

One tool in an AI leader's repertoire to get buy-in for projects, products, and overall change is storytelling. Unlike traditional patterns of telling a story we learn in school, storytelling for business leaders serves a different purpose. Its goal is to convince senior leadership to commit, buy into an idea or proposal, and get relevant information quickly.

Typically, awareness of the subject is essential for making good decisions and understanding a technology's potential. This skill is also known as *AI fluency*. As an AI leader, you have a responsibility and self-interest in helping your peers and teams better understand what AI can do for them and where AI can help them reach or exceed their business goals. With that foundation, you can focus on the following critical aspects for successfully implementing AI in business.

Businesses frequently approach new technologies, such as AI, in the context of projects—whether it is to explore the technology's capabilities, prove its business value, or scale it in production. For example, the all too common aspiration of AI increasing "employee engagement" is an admirable angle, but it will rarely be the sole driver of investment in AI products as these products are expected to deliver measurable business value like any business initiative. This is also a frequent reason why AI fails to deliver on the promise of greater efficiency or higher revenue. When organizations view AI as a product rather than a project, their mindset changes, and they start putting users at the center of their doing rather than timelines and deliverables. Approaching AI as a product also ensures continuous innovation rather than a one-and-done mentality in which a finished project is thrown over the fence to another team that needs to maintain it.

Unless you can measure and quantify the impact on the business, getting stakeholders' buy-in to pursue or continue investing in the idea will be hard. It is also one of the key reasons why users are not adopting AI innovations. Product teams play a pivotal role in the adoption process. They need to understand what AI offers as a technology, which problems it can solve within their product, and which of those features their users even desire. Your role is facilitating this enablement and upskilling so the teams can optimally employ the technology.

As people are the ones who will operate AI-enhanced products, you must design for human-AI collaboration. This design paradigm emphasizes the optimal use of humans' and AI's strengths depending on the task. A formalized process from idea to implementation will help you deliver AI products that provide business value more quickly while offering transparency about the process and progress.

As part of the development and implementation process, AI and business teams must work closely together to ensure the final product meets the business stakeholders' expectations and goals. A proven method for establishing a robust collaboration model is creating a community of multipliers across the organization. In addition to enabling business users to use AI, AI leaders need to upskill their data science and product teams in aspects of the business domain in which they are working. Over time, technical experts can develop an understanding of how their products support the businesses and what business metrics they improve.

Beyond communication between teams, establishing strong guidelines and policies and implementing them is another key aspect of your AI leadership role. During the last AI hype (2016-2020), examples of Machine Learning models that have created biased recommendations emerged. Organizations have increased their efforts to improve AI ethics. As an AI leader, you must define and operationalize principles for using AI in your business.

If AI should serve us all, its predictions and output must also be more inclusive—and so do the teams that are building it. Diversity in thought, ethnic background, gender, and more ensures broad representation. But the reality still looks different. For example, women are underrepresented in data and AI, especially in leadership roles. To change this situation, current leaders need to lead this change, starting with the women who are already in the organization.

In addition to ethics and diversity, sustainability has been gaining traction in connection with AI. For example, LLMs consume significantly more energy than ML models, negatively impacting a company's carbon footprint. But AI has the potential to be a major contributor to increasing social good.

The Generative AI hype gives the impression that you no longer need good data. But the current limitations of LLMs, such as hallucinations and biased output, require you to augment these models with your business data. You can use the following four approaches to generate better output with LLMs: *prompting, Retrieval-Augmented Generation (RAG), knowledge graphs, and fine-tuning.*

A common misconception is that using open-source LLMs leads to lower costs. That incomplete calculation omits infrastructure, maintenance, and enterprise-grade support costs. In addition to the models themselves, open-source components such as tools and UI can be viable alternatives to proprietary options.

The previous approaches and techniques aim at generating more relevant, less biased output. But you can only find out if that is really the case when you evaluate the generated output. Metrics such as *faithfulness* and *toxicity* indicate whether an LLM generates output that is consistent and the language is free of (or low on) harmful aspects.

To mitigate the risk of data leakage to LLM providers, you can use models for inference only, adjust your prompt engineering, use content filtering, or use a local copy of the model in your own cloud environment. Whichever approach you choose, LLMs are subject to a number of vulnerabilities that you need to be aware of to adequately decide where and how to use this technology in your products and mitigate security vulnerabilities such as exfiltrating data or influencing a model's output by injecting hidden information.

Generative AI increases the risk of misinformation as AI-generated information becomes increasingly difficult to distinguish from human-created information. Against this backdrop, the next frontier for AI lies in increasing the autonomy of decision-making, expanding and combining several types of input and processing, and finding robust ways to accelerate its use for good while limiting the potential for misinformation and harm.

Agents can evaluate potential options under uncertainty and reason over the best ones to choose—from individual productivity to business workflows. The range of tasks is broad, going far beyond hardcoded, rule-based automation, enabling entirely new opportunities and further increasing business efficiency.

Given the pace of rapid evolution and change around AI, the majority of approaches and methods outlined in this book will also apply to the next wave of innovation, far beyond AI itself. Those leaders who master AI position themselves well to lead future technology adoptions in business—the next one is just around the corner.

Glossary

Agent: Type of software that can make decisions with limited complexity under multiple conditions while perceiving and manipulating its environment.

AIDA framework (Attention, Interest, Desire, Action): Copywriting framework to structure storytelling that aims at the audience taking a desired action.

Application Programming Interface (API): Software component that allows two or more computer programs to communicate with each other based on defined input and output parameters.

Artificial Intelligence (AI): Umbrella term for software that perceives, decides, and acts based on patterns detected in vast amounts of data; includes Machine Learning, Deep Learning, and Generative AI.

Assistant: Type of software that supports a user in the background by providing feedback and corrections, such as a writing assistant.

BloombergGPT: Fine-tuned LLM by Bloomberg based on financial data for approximately ten million dollars in training cost; outperformed on finance tasks by off-the-shelf OpenAI GPT-4.

Chief Artificial Intelligence Officer (CAIO): C-Suite leadership role tasked with enabling, educating, and leading multi-disciplinary AI efforts within a company.

Chief Data Officer (CDO): C-Suite leadership role primarily focused on ensuring data governance, data quality, and data management in a company.

Chief Digital Officer (CDO): C-Suite leadership role spearheading the digital transformation of a company's business processes and operations.

Chief Financial Officer (CFO): C-Suite leadership role ensuring the financial health of a company.

Chief Information Officer (CIO): C-Suite leadership role leading the IT strategy and operations of enterprise systems that support the business strategy.

Chief Technology Officer (CTO): C-Suite leadership role specializing in the technology strategy of a business.

ChatGPT: Generative AI-based assistant by OpenAI that has quickly gained popularity globally with 100 million users within the first two months.

Center of Excellence (CoE): Team setup for establishing and championing new technology topics within a business.

Copilot: Type of software that executes tasks on the user's behalf in a single domain, such as generating code for a Java application based on user input.

DALL-E: Image generation model by OpenAI.

Deep Learning (DL): AI technique that mimics human-like processing of information via a neural network architecture.

Environmental, Societal, and Governance (ESG): Set of aspects to be considered during investment decisions.

EU AI Act: Regulation defined by the European Union that governs the development and use of AI.

F1-score: Metric of an ML model to identify its quality.

Fear of Missing Out (FOMO): Individual's perception that they (or their business) might be missing out on capitalizing on an opportunity (whether perceived or real).

Fine-Tuning: Process of adapting a foundation model for a specific task based on new data (e.g. see BloombergGPT).

Foundation Model: Type of AI model that can be used for building a wide variety of AI capabilities and products, hence, being used as the foundation of many applications.

Gemini: Family of Generative AI models by Google.

General Data Protection Regulation (GDPR): European Union information privacy and human rights regulation.

Generative AI: Type of AI that generates and output based on submitted input (prompt).

Generative Pre-trained Transformer (GPT): Type of foundation model (Large Language Model) pre-trained on vast amounts of unlabeled data; used to generate human-like output.

Graphics Processing Unit (GPU): Electronic circuit designed to accelerate computer graphics and image processing; used for training neural networks due to parallel processing capability.

Hallucination: Factually incorrect information generated by an LLM.

Information Technology (IT): Domain that includes computer systems, software, programming languages, data, information processing, and storage.

International Organization for Standardization (ISO): Independent, international, non-governmental standard development organization.

Knowledge Cut-Off: Information available to a foundation model until the time of the model's latest training.

Knowledge Graph: Software component that models entities and their relationships; used for knowledge discovery and reasoning over data.

LangChain: Software development and integration framework for building LLM-based applications, such as document analysis, summarization, chatbots, and code analysis.

Large Language Model (LLM): Type of foundation model trained on vast amounts of text and able to generate text based on observed information.

Large Language Model Operations (LLMOps): Process and procedures (operations) of using and providing AI products that incorporate LLMs.

Llama: Family of foundation models by Meta.

LlamaIndex: Data framework for LLM applications to connect custom data sources to LLMs.

Local Interpretable Model-agnostic Explanations (LIME): Technique to explain the prediction of an ML model.

Machine Learning (ML): Subset technology of AI, focused on recognizing (learning) patterns in data.

Midjourney: Image generation model by Midjourney.

Mistral: Generative AI model family by French Generative AI vendor Mistral.

Moonshot: Highly visionary and ambitious projects that challenge the status quo.

Multi-Modal Model: Generative AI model that can process and generate data in multiple types of media, e.g. text, image, audio, or video.

Natural Language: Language that occurs in a human community through use, repetition, and change, such as English, German, Spanish.

Natural Language Processing (NLP): Sub-discipline of AI focused on understanding and generating natural language (e.g. English, German, French).

Off-the-Shelf: Software readily available for use without customization.

Open Source: Software whose source code is openly available for review, modification, and redistribution.

Organization for Economic Co-Operation and Development (OECD): International organization that works to build better policies for better lives.

Personal Identifiable Information (PII): Any information which is related to an identified or identifiable natural person.

Precision: Metric of an ML model to identify the proportion of correctly identified instances.

Prompt: Text-based instruction passed to a Generative AI model upon which the model generates an output.

Prompt Engineering: Emerging software engineering discipline of defining prompts for Generative AI models.

Prompt Injection: Adding information to data that is invisible to humans, but will be interpreted as valid instructions by an LLM.

Recall: Metric of an ML model to identify how often the model correctly identifies positive instances (true positives).

Reinforcement Learning: Method for training ML models and LLMs in which the AI agent receives a reward.

Reinforcement Learning with Human Feedback (RLHF): Method for evaluating the generated output of an LLM; the model predicts how likely a human would validate the generated output as good.

Request for Proposal (RFP): Document used to solicit proposals from potential vendors for a product or service based on the buyer's specifications.

Retrieval-Augmented Generation (RAG): Method for providing data to LLMs that the LLM has not previously been trained on.

Robotic Process Automation (RPA): Technology used to automate and access business processes by recording and simulating (or programming) clicks on a screen as if a user were to execute it.

SHapley Additive exPlanations (SHAP): Technique to explain the prediction of an ML model.

Software-as-a-Service: Delivery model for applications over the internet.

Synthetic Data: Data that has been created in a lab instead of being created through natural observation, events, or transactions.

Token: Unit of measure for determining the input and output of generated information by a foundation model; tokens are often also the pricing metric that platform vendors use for monetization.

Transformer: Deep learning architecture in which text is converted into tokens and converted into a vector.

United Nations Educational, Scientific and Cultural Organization (UNESCO): Specialized agency of the United Nations with the aim of promoting world peace and security through international cooperation in education, arts, sciences, and culture.

User Experience (UX): How a user interacts with and experiences a product, system, or service.

User Interface (UI): Space in which humans interact with a computer or machine.

Appendix

For in-depth context on the topics discussed in this book, please refer to the episodes of *What's the* BUZZ?:
www.intelligence-briefing.com

Episode	Guest	Title	Episode topic
01	Olivier Gomez	CEO & Co-Founder, Intelligent Automation Corp.	Intelligent Automation
02	Doug Shannon	Intelligent Automation Leader	The Path to AI
03	Samuel Best	VP Business Automation, General Motors Financial	Branching Out to AI
04	Emmanuel Lai	Automation Strategist	Running Your First AI Project
05	Ralph Aboujaoude Diaz	Practice Leader, HFS Research	Managing Automation Risks
06	Somil Gupta Kieran Gilmurray	Founder, Algorithmic Scale Author & Digital Transformation Expert	Winning With AI
07	Ariana Smetana Noelle Silver Tolani Jaiye-Tikolo	Digital Transformation Expert AI Ethics & Education Leader Intelligent Automation Expert	The Quest for Trust in AI

08	Sara Hanks	Senior Director Program Management	Top 3 Learnings For New AI Leads
09	Asheesh Biyala	Director Intelligent Automation	The Key to Your Automation Culture
10	Johan Steyn	Professor & Author	A Common Sense Approach for AI
11	Brandon Cosley	Director Artificial Intelligence	Data Science for Non Data Scientists
12	Chris Johannessen	Editor of the Journal of AI, Robotics and Workplace Automation	Setting Up Your AI & Automation CoE
13	Maxim Ioffe	Intelligent Automation Leader, WESCO Distribution	Keep It Pragmatic for Automation & AI
14	Brian Pearce	Senior AI CoE Leader	Leading Your AI CoE To Success
15	Vin Vashishta	AI Strategy Leader	Make Your AI Strategy Actionable
16	Laks Srinivasan	Founder, Return on AI Institute	Increase Business Leaders' AI Fluency
17	Lisa Palmer Debbie Botha Patrick Glauner	Chief AI Strategist, Dr Lisa AI Head of Partnerships, Women in AI Professor, Deggendorf Technical Institute	Opportunity vs Risk? — AI Across Cultures
18	Reid Blackman	Author of "Ethical Machines"	Put AI Ethics Into Practice

19	Vijay Yadhav	Director Quantitative Sciences-Digital, Data & Analytics	Why Your AI Projects Need a Pathfinder
20	Shail Khiyara Frank Casale Ian Barkin	Founder, VOCAL Council Founder, The Institute for RPA & AI Entrepreneur & Investor	AI & Intelligent Automation — What to Expect in 2023
21	Alexander Leonida	Founder, SilkFlo	Automation in a Multi-vendor World
22	Mary Purk	Executive Director, AI & Analytics Center, Wharton School of Business, University of Pennsylvania	Accelerating Your AI Adoption in Business
23	Tom Davenport	Professor & Author	Being "All-In" on Generative AI
24	Amit Arora	VP - Head of Product, Cyber Risk Solutions	Assess Cyber Risk Potential With AI
25	Maya Mikhailov	Founder & AI Leader	Set AI Expectations With Your Leadership
26	Ramsay Brown	Founder & CEO, Mission Control	How Businesses Can Trust Generative AI
27	Brian Evergreen	CEO, The Future Solving Company	Creating a Human Future With AI
28	Rod Schatz	Data & Digital Transformation Executive	Prepare Your Business for AI-Generated Disinformation

29	Ravit Dotan	Director, The Collaborative AI Responsibility Lab at University of Pittsburgh	Define Guardrails for Generative AI in Your Business
30	Aurelie Pols	AI Data Privacy Expert & Advisor	Shape Your Business's Accountability for Generative AI
31	Abi Aryan	Machine Learning & LLMOps Expert	Fine-Tune & Operate Your Generative AI Models
32	Scott Taylor	The Data Whisperer, MetaMeta Consulting	Get Funding for Your AI Projects With Storytelling
33	Supreet Kaur	AI Product Evangelist	Upskill Your Product Team on Generative AI
34	Eric Fraser	Culture Change Executive	Automate Your Job With Generative AI - Fact or Fiction?
35	Ted Shelton	Management Consulting Leader	Keep Your Business Relevant With Generative AI
36	Steve Wilson	Project Leader, OWASP Foundation & Chief Product Officer, Contrast Security	Secure Your LLM Against Common Vulnerabilities
37	Matt Lewis	Chief Artificial and Augmented Intelligence Officer	Grow Your Chief AI Officer Role
38	Harpreet Sahota	Developer Relations Expert	Augment Your Generative AI Model With New Data

39	Tobias Zwingmann	AI Advisor & Author	Build Generative AI Applications With Open Source Tech
40	Keith McCormick	Executive Data Scientist	Build Your AI Team With These Roles
41	Mark Stouse	CEO, Proof Analytics	Teach Your Data Scientists About The Business
42	Enrico Santus	Human-AI Collaboration Leader	Design Human-AI Collaboration for Adaptive Processes
43	Daniel Faggella	Founder, Emerj Research	Generative AI in the Enterprise — Top Trends & Predictions
44	Andrea Isoni	Chief AI Officer	Get Your Business Ready For The EU AI Act
45	Mark Minevich	Chief Digital AI Strategist & Author	Create a Sustainable Future With AI
46	Conor Grennan	Dean of Students, MBA Program & Head of Generative AI, NYU Stern School of Business	Stay on Top of Generative AI Industry News
47	Bill Schmarzo	Professor & Author, Dean of Big Data	Prepare Your Business Teams for Generative AI

48	Scott Clendaniel	VP & AI Instructor, Analytics-Edge	Improve Your User Experience With Generative AI
49	Carly Taylor	Director of Franchise Security Strategy, Activision/ Call of Duty	Strengthen Your Security Against Generative AI Hackers
50	Anthony Alcaraz	Chief Product Officer	Supercharge Your RAG App With a Knowledge Graph
51	Sadie St. Lawrence	Founder, Women in Data & Human-Machine Collaboration Institute	Empower Women to Thrive in Data & AI
52	Bernard Marr	Futurist & Author	Prepare for a Future of Converging Technologies and AI
53	Elizabeth Adams	Leader of Responsible AI	Increase Engagement for Responsible AI Programs
54	Randy Bean	Founder, Data & AI Leadership Exchange	Go Beyond Quick-Win Use Cases for Generative AI
55	Philippe Rambach	Chief AI Officer, Schneider Electric	Drive Sustainability and Energy Efficiency With AI Leadership
56	Kence Anderson	Founder, Composabl	Are Your Agents Ready for Enterprise Decision-Making?

Acknowledgements

Throughout my career, I have been fortunate to work with trusted leaders who have guided me with insight and wisdom. Many of you have become close friends over the years. You have inspired me to pursue leadership roles myself and to become a better leader each day. There has always been a little something that has rubbed off and that I have tried to incorporate into my own leadership when I had the chance to lead—and pay it forward.

This book would not exist if it was not for the AI leaders and practitioners who join me on *What's the* BUZZ? and who share their expertise and experiences with the growing, global community of viewers and listeners. In times of technology hype, you are the voice of reason that helps to cut through the noise. And lastly, a big shout-out to all the current and aspiring AI leaders who are looking for resources to learn about leading AI projects and programs in business. You are well-positioned to spearhead this wave of AI and the next waves of emerging technologies after that. Stay curious—and together, let's turn hype into outcome!

Here's What To Do Next

You have now acquired the foundational knowledge that prepares you to lead AI projects and programs in your business, but AI leadership is constantly evolving!

Whenever you're ready, here are four ways I can help you take the next step on your AI leadership journey:

1. Accelerate Your AI Initiative with Additional Resources

By reading this book and saying yes to yourself, you have unlocked additional resources you can directly use in your AI initiatives.

Visit www.intelligence-briefing.com/resources to leverage a growing repository of resources.

2. Kickstart Your Company's AI Journey

If you found this book helpful and want some help implementing these concepts in your business, I'd love to invite you to chat with me.

Visit www.intelligence-briefing.com/call to schedule a call and discuss your project.

3. Hire Andreas To Speak

If you are looking to inspire your audience at your conference or event with a pragmatic perspective on the state of AI and its opportunities in business, I'd love to bring it!

Email andreas@intelligence-briefing.com with "SPEAKING" in the subject line.

4. Get the Latest Insights to Turn Hype Into Outcome

If you want to stay up to date on leading AI programs in business, subscribe to my newsletter at www.intelligence-briefing.com/newsletter. And of course, you can subscribe to my live stream and podcast, *What's the* BUZZ?, at www.intelligence-briefing.com/podcast to stay up-to-date on the latest topics and trends for AI leaders in business.

Let's keep the conversation going! The journey doesn't end here. I'd love to connect with you and hear about your AI leadership journey.

You can find me on:

- LinkedIn: *https://linkedin.com/in/andreasmwelsch*
- Twitter: *https://twitter.com/andreasmwelsch*
- TikTok: *https://tiktok.com/@intelligencebriefing*
- YouTube: *https://youtube.com/@intelligencebriefing*

Made in the USA
Middletown, DE
04 February 2025